YOUNG PEOPLE'S STORY OF
OUR HERITAGE

YOUNG PEOPLE'S
STORY OF
OUR HERITAGE

THE ANCIENT WORLD

by

V. M. HILLYER and E. G. HUEY

New Edition Designed and Revised by Childrens Press, Chicago

Consultants

William T. Nichol, Principal
Charles Gates Dawes Elementary School, Evanston, Illinois

John R. Lee, Professor of Education
Northwestern University, Evanston, Illinois

Meredith Press, New York

Illustrations in the order in which they appear

Library of Congress Catalog Card Number: 66-11328

Contents

Acknowledgments

Cover drawing: Prehistoric cavemen
John Hollis-Hollis Associates

Cover photograph: **Horsemen,** part of the North Frieze from
the Parthenon in Athens, Greece. British Museum, London.
FPG-Freelance Photographers Guild Inc., New York

Page 2: Neanderthal hunters holding a woolly rhinoceros
at bay.
Field Museum of Natural History

Frontis: Llamas wander among the ruins of Machu Picchu,
an ancient Incan city in the highlands of Peru
Braniff International

Opposite: **Noblewomen,** a detail of an Egyptian mural
painting in a tomb at Thebes, about 1300 B.C.
Historical Pictures Service, Chicago

Designer: John Hollis

Project Editor: Joan Downing

Editorial Staff: Frances Dyra, Mary Reidy, Gerri Stoller

THE ANCIENT WORLD

Prehistory—500 B.C.

Introduction

History is a continuing record of man—his struggles, his achievements, and his failures. It covers a vast—almost unbelievable—period of time, beginning with man's first appearance on earth millions of years ago. In order to present this story more clearly it has been divided into sections. In each section—Ancient, Medieval, and Modern History—we will learn about developments that are as unique and as individual as man himself.

No period covers as long a time as Ancient History. This section begins with cave men and follows man's progress as he develops and learns how to do many things: use fire, plant food, make tools, train and hunt animals, and many other things that simplify and enrich his daily life. This time period, because it comes before the development of writing, is called *prehistory*, or *prehistoric time*. Our knowledge and understanding of this age is based on the physical things left behind. These include tools, cave homes, art, and even skeletons. All these things tell us what we know about early man and his life.

Historic time, or recorded time, begins only about six thousand years ago, with the first system of writing. With written records, of course, our knowledge of what went on during a certain period increased. We can see clearly how man created ways of keeping order through his leaders, his government, and his rules or laws; how everyday life was made easier with every new invention and discovery; and how man satisfied and increased his understanding of the world through his studies, religion, literature, and art. Each nation—whether it was Egyptian, Sumerian, Persian, Indian, Greek, or Roman— grew from a simple farm-based life to a big, complicated, and important nation. Each has left a record of accomplishments that is as special as man himself. Each was built on some part of an earlier civilization, but went beyond it.

Because Ancient History covers such a very long period of time it has been divided into two books. The first one, which covers from prehistoric time to 500 B.C., will show how man developed from cave life to the city life found around the Mediterranean Sea—in Egypt, Crete, Greece.

The second book will discuss the highpoints of life during the period of later Ancient History—the cultural, governmental, and social achievements and refinements found in the civilizations of Greece and Rome.

Ancient History is a true story of war, of peace, of great leaders, and of wicked men. It tells of the rich and the poor, the good and the bad, who are found in every nation's history.

Men of the
Old Stone Age
tending their
fire

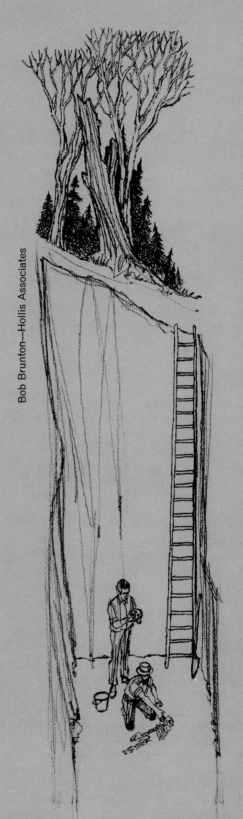

left: The skull and head of Neanderthal Man (top) and Cro-Magnon man (bottom) as restored by Dr. J. H. McGregor

above: Archaeologists spend much time digging for clues to past history

The Earliest Man

Every story has a beginning. Since history is the story of mankind, it has a beginning, too. But no one knows exactly what that beginning was like, or when it happened, because the people who lived then left no written records to tell us about it. This time before the development of writing is called *prehistoric time*, or prehistory.

If you were going to read the story of mankind beginning only with the written records left by ancient peoples it would be like starting in the middle of a book, and you probably would not like a story like that.

Other people didn't like it either, and some of them looked for unwritten records that can tell about very early man—*prehistoric man*.

Prehistory covers millions of years. History, written records, covers only about 6,000 years. Prehistory goes all the way back to the time when there were no men on the planet we call earth. That was millions and millions of years ago, during the time when the earth was forming and the plants and animals began to appear. Man is a newcomer to earth. He appeared only about one million years ago.

If early man left no written records, how do we know that he was even here at that time? What kind of records can we possibly find that tell he existed?

These unwritten records consist mainly of man's own remains, or skeletons, which show his size and appearance, and the remains of the things he made. The things he made and left behind are called *artifacts*. These include many different tools and weapons. Artifacts are very important because, where there are artifacts, there was once man. This man could use his mind to figure out ways of making his life easier.

The earliest man we know about—*Neanderthal man* (nee-an'der-thal)—did not look like the men of today. We know this from the parts of skeletons found. Neanderthal man was a short, thick-set person who walked with bent knees and stooped forward. Apparently he was very strong. His jaw was heavy and he had a chin that must have made talking very difficult. His forehead was low and receding.

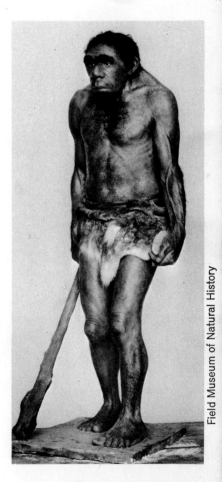

Neanderthal man with his primitive weapons

Field Museum of Natural History—Sculptor, Frederick Blaschke

Neanderthal family
of Gibralter
tend the fire
just outside
their cave home

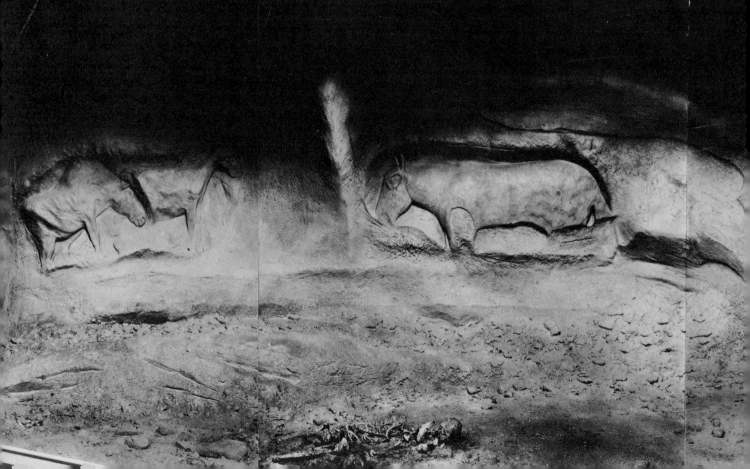

Although Neanderthal men did not seem to be very advanced, they did make very simple tools and weapons. They did not build houses, but lived in caves to escape the cold weather that winter brought to northern Europe, where they lived. Neanderthal man seems to have lived well enough about 75,000 or 150,000 years ago, until Cro-Magnon (crow-mag'nun) man moved into northern Europe from the south. When this happened, Neanderthal man seems to have disappeared. He may have been killed by Cro-Magnon man, but we are not sure.

Cro-Magnon man was much more like men of today. He made better tools and weapons. He did something else, too, that was very different and tells us much about him. On the walls of caves he drew and painted pictures of the animals he knew. These have been found in France and Spain. He used artistic ability to express what he saw about him. Modern man has been able to learn much from these paintings that form a new and important record of the ancient times. They tell modern man many things he wants to know about Cro-Magnon man.

Very early man, the kind who came before even Neanderthal man, had been very dependent on his immediate surroundings —his *environment.* That means that like the wild animals, he had taken his food from his surroundings and had moved with the sun. He had no need to grow anything, for he lived off the land and ate whatever he found. He lived outdoors and did not worry about what the next day would bring. Everything was very pleasant indeed, until the earth grew very cold and big sheets of ice known as *glaciers* came moving down upon him from the north. Things were no longer pleasant, and man had to find new kinds of food to eat and new ways and places to shelter himself. He was further troubled when the weather brought first too much rain and then *drought—* no rain at all.

These extremes in environment, or surroundings, occurred on earth several times in the very early centuries of man's existence. He had to get used to it—*adapt*—or die. He had to learn to live in these new surroundings, or find other surroundings. Early man solved his problem by moving away from the severe cold and rain and the very dry places. He moved very great distances. That is how the race of man became scattered all over the earth. Since he had no boats or car, early man had

opposite top: Prehistoric man draws on the walls of his cave

opposite bottom: Sculptures also were carved on cave walls

above: A Paleolithic painting of a bison found in a cave in France

17

opposite top: Wild boar hunted by prehistoric man in western Europe

opposite bottom: Woolly rhinoceros

left: Prehistoric bear hunters prepare to stone their prey

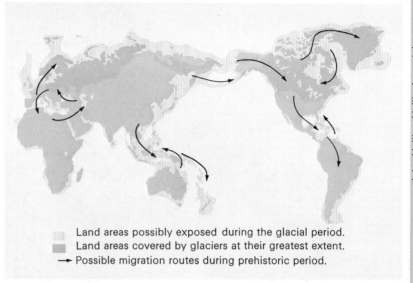

John Hollis—Hollis Associates

Land areas possibly exposed during the glacial period.
Land areas covered by glaciers at their greatest extent.
→ Possible migration routes during prehistoric period.

above right: Map of the world showing glaciers, possible land bridges during the glacier periods, and probable migration routes of early man

to travel by foot. How could he then, have gone from one continent to another? How could he cross oceans and seas?

Hundreds of thousands of years ago, the land surfaces of the earth were not as they are now. Geologists, scientists who study the earth and its history, say there were *land bridges* connecting the various continents with one another. These were much like the land bridge of Central America that connects the continents of North and South America. Some early people walked over these land bridges to get away from the bad weather. But during the long period of time they were away from their original home, the earth changed again and many of these land bridges disappeared. People could not get back to where they had come from, and so they stayed in the new place.

Finally after many, many generations had come and gone, no one was left who could tell his own people where they had first lived. Everyone forgot that there were other continents besides theirs. This is how people who had traveled to escape the severe weather established whole new groups in very different environments. Some people think that is why there are different races of mankind today. They think that those who went to Asia became the Mongoloid race; those who went to Africa became the Negroid race; those who went to America became Indians; and those who lived in western Asia, Europe, and North Africa became the Caucasoid race.

These people do look different from one another today certainly. The color of their skin is different, and the texture of their hair and the shape of their heads are all different. But just how and why it came to be that way is still not certain.

The Stone Age

Both Neanderthal man and Cro-Magnon man lived during the Old Stone Age, which is the earliest age of prehistory. The age gets its name from the fact that during that time, man made his tools and weapons from stone. Then he did not know about other materials, such as metal. The Old Stone Age, which is also called the *Paleolithic Age* (pay-lee-oh-lith′ihk) began about 500,000 B.C. or 500,000 years before the birth of Christ.

The initials "B.C." mean "before Christ." Many people in the world today call the year that Christ was born "year one." Everything that happened before that time is said to be "before Christ." Everything that has happened in the world since that time is said to have happened "in the year of Our Lord." This is written *Anno Domini* in Latin. An abbreviation "A.D.," often is placed with the number of the year. So if something happened one thousand years after the birth of Christ, we write the date as A.D. 1000 or 1000 A.D. But most of the time we write just the year, 1000 without using the initials. If no initials are written before or after the year number, the time meant is *after* Christ's birth, or A.D. If the time is *before* Christ's birth, however, the initials "B.C." are *always* used.

Nearly everything we discuss in this book happened before the birth of Christ. So "B.C." will appear after nearly every year number. Remember that to find out just how long ago a "B.C." year was, you must count the number of years that have passed since the birth of Christ and add them to the year number given. You are living in the twentieth century, which means that you are living more than 1900 years since Christ was born. If you read this book in 1970, then you add 1970 years to the date that is given with the "B.C." after it. Now you can see that the Old Stone Age, that began in 500,000 B.C. really began more than 501,900 years ago.

Things were very different then from what they are now, but men were beginning to invent and to discover many important things. The first stone implements were very crude. They are called *eoliths* (ee′oh-liths), which means "drawn

above: A Paleolithic hand-ax measuring about ten inches

stones." Eoliths were pieces of stone that had been broken or chipped in a way that would make them useful. Much later, man learned how to shape the stone into the tool he wanted. The first tool of the Old Stone Age was a hatchet, or hand-ax. It was not like any hatchet or any ax used today. At first it did not have a handle, but was only a large piece of stone from four to ten inches long. It had one sharp edge for cutting, and one rounded edge for holding. Such a tool may not seem very wonderful to us, but making it was an important first step for man to have taken. Though it was the only tool he made for thousands of years, at least he was starting to be a craftsman.

It was during the Old Stone Age that Cro-Magnon man learned to create fire by friction. Before that time, man had to count on nature to make a fire for him. He then had to tend it carefully to keep it alive for his own use. With the discovery of a way to create fire, early man was able to move about more, for he always had his fire source with him.

The Old Stone Age ended in different parts of the world at different times. Probably the earliest end of the Old Stone Age was about 10,000 B.C. Then the New Stone Age, or *Neolithic Age* (nee-oh-lith'ik), began. Neolithic comes from the Greek words *neo* (new) and *lithic* (stone).

Man's life had changed quite a lot by then. He had become an advanced craftsman and could make many special tools. He had learned how to attach a handle to the hand-ax so he could strike more powerful blows with it. Then he developed spears and bows and arrows that enabled him to kill food animals from a safe distance. These weapons also helped protect him from enemies in ways other than hand-to-hand combat. When he developed *scrapers* and *awls*, man could prepare animal skins to use for his clothing. Neolithic man made special tools for special projects.

By this time man's life had changed in other ways. He had now become a farmer and a villager. Just exactly when man began to leave his wandering and hunting way of life is not certain, but by the time of the New Stone Age, he had developed village communities, tamed horses to ride, and domesticated (tamed) such farm animals as cows. He tilled the soil and grew his food. He was no longer dependent only on what might come his way through the forest in time for dinner.

Cavemen hunted
and killed wild bulls

In order to become a farmer, one must be able to settle down in one place and work the soil with advanced tools. Thus, as might be expected, the New Stone Age was the time for the development or invention of tools more complicated than stick tools. During this age the wooden plow and the sickle were invented and used.

Community effort was needed to maintain a village. To make successful the more complicated lives that the men of the New Stone Age began to live, there had to exist some form of language and a system for passing on knowledge. Just how that language developed is not known. Neanderthal man probably had some form of language communication, although many believe that it was no more than a system of grunts and groans. With Cro-Magnon man, the language probably improved. New Stone Age man must have had some rather complicated form of speech to express his knowledge and his needs.

The co-operative living necessary to village life also made some specialization of work necessary. Without help, a man cannot farm, herd his cattle, and make all of his own tools, clothing, and shelter. So man learned to trade some of his time and talent for things his neighbor could supply.

This communication among men and sharing and exchanging of products did not stop at the boundaries of the ancient villages. Artifacts known to have been made by one group of people have been found in areas where we know these people did not live. This shows us that New Stone Age man traveled from place to place, and perhaps even did some trading with people who lived a great distance from his own village. He may have traveled on foot, but he probably did some exploring in crude boats and on horseback.

Since New Stone Age man had developed a language, when he traveled he could bring with him ideas as well as tools and weapons. He could distribute knowledge to others and gain new knowledge from them as well. Man learned to co-operate with people in his own village and also with those in other villages.

This co-operation was natural to man. The first co-operative move in a person's life comes when he is a baby. He belongs to a family and must live in the group that makes up this family when he is young, or he will die for want of food, clothing, shelter, and protection. The community is like a bigger family. Therefore, it is not a strange thing to man at all.

As long as man was a wanderer and a hunter, he lived in the small family group, but when he became a landholder, he needed to be surrounded by many more people. One thing that makes it difficult for large numbers of men to live together successfully is the fact that men are individuals with many differences. In order to lessen these differences, communities of men began to do things in the same way and so developed *customs*. They also began to judge what was good and what was bad for their way of life. The things that were bad, such as stealing, were forbidden, or *taboo*.

There were no policemen in the New Stone Age to see that people did not do things that were taboo. Custom was so strong that the people themselves seemed to obey it without policemen. Of course, the rules were simple and there were not very many of them. They could be learned early in life and could be remembered easily, which probably helped people follow them without being forced to do so.

left: Reconstruction of a
Swiss Lake village

Although the New Stone Age men had advanced tools and lived in communities, all men were not alike in everything they did. Some continued to make hunting their main source of wealth. Others counted on farming. Where they lived made a big difference in what they did. For example, the Alpine branch of the Caucasoid race were still a hunting people, even though they lived in villages and did other kinds of work, too. Some of them built special kinds of villages and houses on lakes. They are called *lake dwellers.*

These people lived in what is now Switzerland. They built houses and walks on top of large poles, or piles, which they drove into the ground beneath the water. To be able to build such structures on piles took co-operation among the people who would live this way, and also required knowledge of engineering. These Swiss lake dwellers had to be very intelligent to figure out how to live on water. We do not really know why they decided to live on the lakes, but it probably was for protection from big animals, or even from other men who were not friendly.

We know how the lake dwellers lived because we have found ruins of their villages and many artifacts and other remainders of their lives. From these things we know they were great hunters, and that they also were farmers. They had domesticated such animals as sheep, pigs, and cattle. They had domesticated dogs as well, probably for both work and play.

Swiss Lake Dweller
fishermen haul
in their catch

Their clothing was made well. From the sheep they got wool to make woolen cloth. They also grew flax for linen cloth. Weaving, therefore, was among their accomplishments.

All people of the New Stone Age knew how to make pottery. We know this because archaeologists have found so many pieces of pottery in various places in the world. They have been able to date it back to New Stone Age times more than 11,000 years ago. Some people believe that early man first learned to make pottery by using mud to fill in holes in baskets. Later, they say, these men discovered that clay was the best kind of material to use and that baking the clay would make it stronger and longer lasting.

New Stone Age man not only learned to make pottery utensils to hold water and other liquid, but also he learned how to shape these utensils in various ways. When he became very good at his craft, he even had fashions in pottery— special shapes and designs. Just as people do today, he would discard the old for the newer up-to-date model.

With the New Stone Age, man had begun to use his own intelligence to make for himself what he needed but could not find easily. But there were still many things that could defeat him. The rain he needed for his crops might not come, for instance. Lightning might destroy his house and fire could kill everything around him. These things could happen any time, and man did not have any control over them. These powers of nature at first were noticeable because they were destructive. Man feared them and wondered how to escape them. They seemed to be unfriendly spirits beyond his understanding.

Eventually, man decided that if there were unfriendly spirits, perhaps there also were friendly ones, or perhaps those who were unfriendly could somehow be made otherwise. Some men seemed to know more than others about the wishes of these spirits; they seemed to know how to make them friendly. These were the *medicine men;* they suggested that if their neighbors performed certain rites or ceremonies, the spirits would be pleased and would help them.

From this simple beginning, New Stone Age man developed *gods* who were like the sun or lightning or some other thing that he knew from the nature that was around him. He believed there was a sun-god, a rain-god, a moon-god, and many, many others. Thus he had a primitive religion. It was based on superstition and fear, but it was very real and important to him. The idea of there being one god only was not to occur to man until much later.

above: Artifacts of the Swiss Lake Dwellers

opposite top: Glazed pottery

opposite bottom: Neolithic Sun-worship

Metal Becomes Man's Servant

Although New Stone Age man in many ways was far ahead of Old Stone Age man, he was far from forming a civilization. About 4000 B.C. however, the people who lived in western Asia and Egypt did learn how to work with copper. This first big step toward the development of civilization was the beginning of what we call the Copper Age. It lasted until about 3000 B.C.

How did people discover how to use copper? Remember that the people of the Stone Age had never seen or heard of such a thing as iron or steel, tin or brass, or any metal at all. They made all their tools and weapons from stone and sticks and other materials they found. Then one day a Stone Age man made an accidental discovery.

He made a fire and then put some rock around it to make a kind of campfire stove. It happened that the particular rock he was using was *ore*—rock that contained metal. But this rock did not have just any kind of metal in it, it had copper.

The heat of the fire melted some of the copper, which ran onto the ground. These drops of copper were bright and shiny, so the man noticed them. He examined them and heated more of the ore and got more copper. He had discovered two things. He had discovered metal and he had discovered how to take it out or extract it from ore.

Since he had a new material—and a pretty one at that—he wanted to find a way to use it. At first, he used the copper for beads and other ornaments. But soon people found that they could pound the copper into shapes to make utensils such as pots and pans. But still they had to use stone for tools and weapons that had to be hard and rigid, for copper itself was too soft to be used for spearheads and knives.

The next metal discovered probably was *tin*. Man found that he could use this metal in much the same way that he used copper. But he learned something else, too—something even more important. He discovered that if he mixed the copper and the tin together he got *bronze*, and bronze is a very hard metal. Now he had a material that was even better than stone for making spearheads and knives. For about two thousand years people made their tools and weapons of bronze. We call the time when men used bronze tools and bronze weapons the *Bronze Age*. That probably lasted until 1000 B.C.

When men learned to combine copper and tin, he had learned to make *alloys*. An alloy is any material made up of two or more metals, or a metal and something else that combines to make a new substance. Ores are not alloys, because the metal in ore is not really a part of the stone. It does not really change

the stone but just lies inside it. Alloys are very important to modern man. He could not make his space craft work if it were not for alloys. Sterling silver spoons would not hold their shape if it were not for alloys, for pure silver is very soft. Something else has to be put into it to make it hard.

The alloy known as bronze was a wonderful material for man. But his discoveries did not end there. About 1000 B.C. he discovered *iron*. This marked the beginning of the *Iron Age* which is still going on. You will realize the importance iron has today if you remember that steel is made from it. All the big skyscrapers are made from steel. Some cooking pots and electric fans, and many many other things that you use every day are made from steel.

People who had bronze and iron were able to do many things they could not possibly have done with only stone. They lived much more as we do now. We call the people of the Bronze and Iron Ages *civilized*.

above left: Bronze swords and daggers

---

above: Copper bowl with a handle

31

Where Civilization First Began

People of the Bronze Age and the early Iron Age thought the world was flat. They knew only a small part of the world—the part where they lived. They thought that if you went too far away, the world came to an end and you could tumble off. They knew, however, that there was other land on this flat world. This faraway land that no one had ever seen was called the *Ultima Thule*, which means something like "at the end, in the north."

Today men know that the world is round. Men in space crafts have gone round and round the earth and have taken pictures of it showing exactly how it looks. To find out how the place looked where civilization first began, let's pretend that we are looking down at that spot from a space ship. It would be a very small spot in terms of the size of the whole earth. To get a really good picture of the details of the landscape, we would need a very special camera. The lens would have to make everything look hundreds and hundreds of times bigger than what we could see with the naked eye. But if we did have such a camera we could take a picture that would look something like the drawing showing Mesopotamia and the Mediterranean Sea.

Can you see the land, three rivers, four seas, and a gulf? Look at the names. You may never have heard of some of these places. But they have been known longer than any other place in the world. One of the rivers is the Tigris (ty′gris). You can remember that name because it sounds like the word for a female tiger. Another one is the Nile. That is a short name and is pronounced like the word mile except that the first letter is an "n" instead of an "m." This is a very long river, that travels for miles and miles. The third river is the Euphrates (you-fray′teez).

The Tigris and Euphrates run through the land getting closer and closer together until at last they meet each other and flow into what is called the Persian Gulf. The Nile River flows into the Mediterranean Sea (mehd-ih-teh-ray′nee-an). During the Bronze Age the land that was between the Tigris River and the Euphrates River was called Mesopotamia (mess-oh-poh-tay′mee-ah). The land along the Nile River was

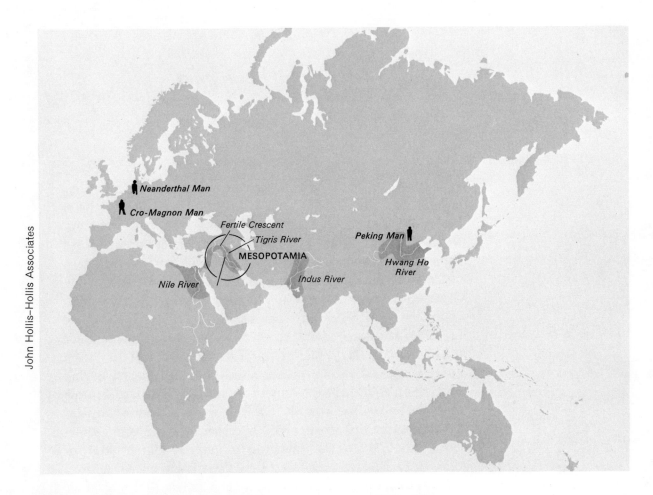

John Hollis–Hollis Associates

Egypt (ee′gihpt). The word "Mediterranean" means "in the middle of the land." You can see why this sea has such a name. It is surrounded by land.

The civilized nations of the Bronze Age that we know most about lived along the Nile in Egypt and along the Tigris and Euphrates in Mesopotamia. There may have been cavemen living in other parts of the world during the Bronze Age, but it is only of the people in these two places—Egypt and Mesopotamia—that we have any written history.

All the people who lived in the country of the Tigris and Euphrates were *Caucasian*. There were, we think, just three different types of Caucasian families there. The names of these three families are Semite (sehm′ite), Hamite (ham′ite), and an Indo-European group called Aryan (air′ee-yuhn).

above: While the remains of early man have been found in Europe, Africa, and the Orient, the important early civilizations thrived in the temperate, fertile river valleys

33

Real History Begins

In the early part of this book, you remember, we said that *history* had to come from written records. Up to now, we have been talking about *prehistory*, the time before there were any written records. Now we will talk about times for which we have some written records.

This, of course, does not mean that we know everything there is to know about what happened since the time man first started writing. Many things that were written down have been lost or destroyed and so we have never seen them. Other records are not very long or complete. We still use unwritten records to give us more clues about what happened during many periods of history. Sometimes we use unwritten records to test the written records, for the written records are not always as truthful as we would like them to be. People sometimes add to a story or change it to make it sound better, or they write it or tell it the way they *think* it happened. A story that is told to many people who then tell it to many other people, usually changes quite a lot. If the last person to hear it writes it down it usually is so different from the way it was first told that the person who told it first wouldn't recognize it!

You can see how this happens by playing a game. Ask a group of your friends to sit in a row. Then have the first person in the row make up a short story of just a few sentences and whisper it to the next person so that no one else can hear it. That person, in turn, should whisper the story to the next person and then he, in turn, should whisper it to the next one. When the last person in the row has heard the story, he should tell it out loud to everyone else. You will be surprised how the story has changed, even though everyone has tried to repeat it just as he heard it.

You can see from this game that stories have a way of getting changed. If we are to believe them, then, we need to have more than just one person's view of it. History is complicated, and so of course we need as much information as we can get from as many good sources as we can find if we are to know what did happen.

The people who write history books get the story from different books. They check all the facts to see if all the books agree before they write them down for you to read. If they do not have more than one source of information, however, then they are careful to tell you that something happened "probably" in a certain way and at "about" a certain time.

We can use 3400 B.C. as the first real date in history, although it is arrived at through some guesswork. A long time after this date, a man in Egypt, the country along the Nile, wrote about a king named Menes (mee'neez). From some of the things the writer said, we are fairly sure that Menes was the king of Egypt in 3400 B.C.

If Menes was a king, then that means he had a kingdom. He must have had subjects and a whole country with many villages and much activity. How did this kingdom happen to be in Egypt and who were the people who lived in it?

The first history that we feel fairly sure is true begins with the Hamite family. The Hamites, you remember, were one of the three families who lived near the Tigris and Euphrates. We think they moved away from these rivers and went down to Egypt long before recorded history began.

Of course, they did not pack all of their furniture on a big wagon and move to Egypt, as you might move from the house where you now live to another. They lived in tents then and not in houses at all, and they moved only one day's journey at a time.

When they got tired of one place or had eaten up everything there was nearby, they rolled up their tents, packed them on camels, and moved a little farther along to the next good place. At last they came to the land we call Egypt. When they reached Egypt, they found it such a fine country in which to live that they stayed there for good. When they got there they found other people already living in the valley. We do not know who they were or from where they came. The Hamites lived among them and married them. The descendents of the two peoples became the very early Egyptians.

Why do you suppose Egypt was such a fine country in which to live? It was mainly because the river Nile flooded the country once a year. It rained so hard every spring in certain places along the river that streams of water flowed into the Nile and made the river overflow its banks. This was not just a little flood, nor was it a flood that lasted for only a little while. The flood was so great that the whole Nile Valley—the river and the land on both sides of it—became covered with water. It formed a kind of lake that was more than ten miles wide and six hundred miles long! Little by little, the water drained into the earth, or, finally, to the Mediterranean Sea. Every year the flood lasted from June until November.

Something more than just water came to the land during these floods. When the rain began, rich soil was carried away by the streams of water into the flooded Nile. The river left this soil along its banks as it rushed through the land. So after the flood had gone down, there was wonderful rich, wet soil waiting to be cultivated and planted. In that fertile soil there grew food and plants of all kinds, and the really wonderful thing about it was that after one year's crop had been harvested, the Nile made the soil rich again for yet another year's crop.

The people today take advantage of this wonder of nature. Aswan Dam and other modern dams control the Nile's annual flood. These dams hold back the water. At Aswan more than 600,000 gallons are held in a reservoir and released when needed. So Egyptians can grow and harvest two, or even three, crops in a year.

The Nile has done something else that rivers do not usually do for a country. It has made Egypt longer than it once was. Some of the soil carried by the river is not left along the banks but goes all the way to the river's mouth. It builds up there and forms a triangular piece of land, called a delta (dell'tah). This delta covers an area of 10,000 miles!

In the United States, the Mississippi River has built up a delta in the state of Louisiana. The Mississippi acts something like the Nile in Egypt, although not on such a giant scale.

If it were not for this yearly overflow of the Nile, the country of Egypt would be a sandy desert in which no plant or living thing would grow. Egypt without water would be like the great Sahara Desert, which is not far away. It is the Nile,

Development of agriculture
along the Nile River

therefore, that makes the land of Egypt rich. It is a good country in which to live, for food grows easily and costs almost nothing. Besides this, the climate is so warm that people need little clothing and do not have to buy coal or make fires to heat their houses.

Since food was so easy to get in that land and since shelter and clothing were not problems either, the early people who lived there could turn their attention to other things. They built one of the first great civilizations we know about.

Like other people who lived during the Copper Age and afterward, the very early Egyptians got their food by hunting, fishing, and farming. The crops they raised gave them material for cloth, such as cotton and linen. These people in Egypt built houses, but because the climate was so warm, the houses were light and flimsy. They were made of the materials the people could find around them—mainly mud and bunches of reeds.

The houses kept out the cold night air and gave shade during the day—two things that were very important in Egypt. The people did not have to worry about rain because there was none. The heavy rains that flooded the Nile fell a long way from where the Egyptians lived. But the nights became cold. Egypt has a desert climate and although deserts become very hot during the day, they are very cold at night.

These early Egyptians developed a complex language early in their civilization. And they began to develop a form of writing. Their writing was not made up of letters of the alphabet, but of pictures. This picture writing was called hieroglyphics (hy-roh-glif′iks). This word means "sacred writing"; Egyptian writing was named that because at the beginning the written language was used only for religious things.

The very early forms of Egyptian picture writing were series of little sketches of birds, lions, spears, whips, and other things from everyday life. This kind of writing takes up much more space than most writing today.

The Egyptian system of writing did not develop quickly and it did not remain the same. At first, if a person wanted to write a word for bird, he drew a picture of a whole bird. If he wanted to write a word for fish, he drew a picture of a whole fish.

There was a separate picture for everything. Imagine how hard it must have been to learn. Thousands of symbols, or pictures, had to be memorized—each one different from all the rest.

Because it was so difficult, very few Egyptians learned to write. People called *scribes* were the official writers in Egypt and did the writing for those who did not know how. After

A list of slaves on a plaster cast of the oldest writing ever discovered. (From about 4000 B.C.)

37

many hundreds of years, the scribes discovered a quicker and easier way to do the writing. Instead of making whole pictures, they made only part of the picture to represent the thing. For the word "house" they no longer drew the whole house, but only the four walls of the house. The result was the same. The word "house" was written, but the new "short-hand" kind of writing was easier to write and to read.

Hundreds of years after that, the scribes noticed something about writing that would make it still easier. Many Egyptian words are like one another. That is, some of their parts, called syllables, are exactly the same. The scribes began to make pictures for these syllables instead of for whole words. For example, the picture of a mouth at first stood for the word "mouth." But the Egyptian word for mouth was *ro*, and in this last stage of Egyptian writing the picture of a mouth stood for the sound "r." The scribes wrote a word by drawing the pictures for the syllables that made up the word. This was much easier, for they did not need to use so many separate pictures.

The Egyptians eventually made up pictures for all the consonant sounds. They didn't use pictures for vowel sounds because they could tell when reading something what the vowels were supposed to be. There were twenty-four consonant sound signs in all. This was a *phonetic alphabet*, the earliest known kind of alphabet. It was used as early as 3500 B.C. Now they were getting close to the kind of writing that is done today. But for some reason, the scribes did not use writing that was made up of letter symbols. They still used picture symbols.

Some other people realized how important the writing with letters could be. The Phoenicians (fih-nee'shunz) used the sound symbols of the Egyptians to make their own letter signs, and then passed them on to the Greeks. It was the Greeks who finally made up our system of writing. You will hear more about both of these people, the Phoenicians and the Greeks, later in this book.

The Egyptians did some of their writing on the walls of tombs, but most of it was done on a material the Egyptians invented. It was made from the *papyrus* plant, which was a river reed. When this was split in two, pounded, and rubbed smooth, it was something like very fine parchment, a kind of pale yellow paper that is used even today. The English word "paper" comes from the word "papyrus."

left: A hieroglyphic papyrus, part of a chapter from the Book of the Dead. Copies of this book, which contained special prayers, were placed in Egyptian tombs.

This papyrus paper was very strong, but that is not the main reason why it has lasted for thousands of years. The climate of Egypt is very dry, and things in a very dry climate do not crumble away as fast as things in a wet climate might. So some of the ancient Egyptian writing on papyrus remains even today.

The Egyptians did not make books of their papyrus writings. They made scrolls, which are not as convenient to read as books. The Egyptians used black ink and colored ink to write with. These inks were very much like the inks we use today. The black ink was made from soot and vegetable gum. The colored ink was made from special colored powders.

The early Egyptians, like some other early people, had an organized religion. Remember we said that some of the writings were found on the walls of tombs? These tombs were great structures in which the Egyptians buried some of their most important people. They have become a history lesson in stone and one of the most important sources of information about life in early Egypt.

The Egyptians believed in many spirits. They believed that each man and each animal had a spirit within his body. They thought also that spirits lived in other things as well. They prayed to many gods, and they made idols of them. Every little village had its own special gods. Added to them were the major gods that all of the people from all of the villages believed in. The Egyptians believed that if the gods were kept happy, natural things would turn out all right. They placed food and drink before the images of the gods to help keep them happy. Apparently some animals were sacred. Embalmed bodies of bulls and gold and silver ornaments in the shape of cats have been found.

The people worshipped in special buildings and had priests who told them of the will of their gods. The priests were very powerful in Egypt because they were believed to be the only ones who knew how to keep the gods happy. The people of the land spent a large portion of their time keeping the priests themselves happy and well fed. A generous share of their crops was given to the priests. Besides being the religious authorities, the priests usually were scribes, too, and did most of the writing. They were the educated men of Egypt.

The Egyptians believed in life after death—that a person's spirit lived on even after he died. They thought he would continue to do the same things in this "after life" that he did before he died; therefore, they believed he would need the same things he needed during his lifetime. Because of this, when the important people died and were placed in tombs, they were surrounded by all the things they needed for living. Furniture, vases, cooking pots, and food were placed in the tombs. And statues of animals were placed in the tombs as well.

Often the walls of the tomb were covered with picture writing that told of what the person had done during his lifetime or what great events had happened while he was alive. Papyrus scrolls might also be placed in the tomb. On them would be prayers for the spirit of the dead person, or "Ka" as the Egyptians called the spirit.

Egyptians believed that the body had to be kept from decay; that otherwise the person could not have a life after death. The very early way of preparing the body for burial was to dry it out and protect it with a tomb. Much later the Egyptians learned to embalm the bodies of the dead to further preserve them. These remains we call *mummies*. They tell us much about how the people looked—how tall they were, for example —and how advanced they were in preserving things.

Bronze figure of
Egyptian god

Egypt – the Old Kingdom

Historians usually divide the history of Egypt into three periods—*the Old Kingdom, the Middle Kingdom,* and *the New Kingdom*. Egyptian life was not really divided like this, of course; people in ancient Egypt probably did not think of themselves as living in any particular time in history. But to make it easier for us to understand what was going on and how the civilization advanced, we will divide our discussion of the long years of Egyptian civilization in this way.

The first period was the time of the Old Kingdom, from about 3400 B.C. to 2200 B.C. The second was the time of the Middle Kingdom, from 2200 B.C. to 1800 B.C. The third period was the time of the New Kingdom, from about 1600 B.C. to 1100 B.C. The years between 1800 B.C. and 1600 B.C. are not included in these dates for the Egyptian kingdoms. During those 200 years the ancient Egyptians were in the hands of an enemy— the Hyksos (hick'sose)—who conquered them in a war.

We do not know very much about the Hyksos. We do know they used horses to pull chariots, which were like little plat- forms on wheels. They also had a new kind of curved weapon that worked like a sword. It was called a *scimitar* (sihm'ih-tahr) and was made of bronze. These two things, the chariot and the scimitar, made all the difference to the outcome of the battle with the Egyptians.

The Hyksos were good warriors, but they were not very good at running a country. Besides, there were not nearly as many Hyksos in Egypt as there were Egyptians. When the Egyptians had learned how to make chariots and drive them, and how to make scimitars and use them, they finally took their country back from the Hyksos. But it took them about 200 years to do these things.

You remember that a man named Menes was the first king of Egypt that we know very much about; and you remember that he lived about 3400 B.C. Because he was the first one we know much about, we say that the Old Kingdom began with him. There were kings before him, of course, and they may have been very important, but we don't really know what they did.

We do know that Menes did at least one thing that was very important. He united all Egypt. Until his time, Egypt had been divided into the *Upper Kingdom* and the *Lower Kingdom*. The words "upper" and "lower" describe where the lands were in relation to the Mediterranean Sea. The Lower Kingdom was in the land nearest the delta, the land near the Mediterranean Sea. The Upper Kingdom was the land farthest from the delta.

We do not know how Menes united the country or exactly how many kings had ruled his territory before him. But we do know that there had been thirty dynasties (dye'neh-steez) before him. Dynasty is the word used to describe all the kings of one family. Before Menes, thirty families—one after another —had ruled his territory.

We know about the thirty dynasties from the writings left by the scribe who wrote about Menes and the time before him. The written record mentions time, which is how we were able to determine when Menes ruled. In order for the scribe to have been able to mention time, he must have known how to figure time. The Egyptians therefore, must have had a calendar. Figuring out a calendar is a hard thing to do. But the Egyptians did it. Just as they discovered a way to write their language, they also figured out a way to keep track of time. That was a great advancement, and a lucky one for us.

When Menes became king he wore a double crown to show that he ruled both halves of Egypt—Upper Egypt and Lower Egypt. Menes was in a very good position for a ruler. His country had been building a great civilization for a long time before he was born. Besides that, the people believed that their kings were the direct descendents of their chief god. That meant the kings were divine. They were gods. They were half men and half god to their people. So they took the name "pharaoh" (fay'ro), which means "great house." The pharaoh was so holy that people didn't use his name when talking about him. They respectfully used this word only, which was the name of his house or palace.

Now if you were a king, you would have much power. People would do what you said because you were king. But people might also decide that you were really not much better than they were and someone might try to take your throne away from you. Another person might think that he had as much right to be king as you had. But if you could convince him that you were not just a man, that you were really a god, he

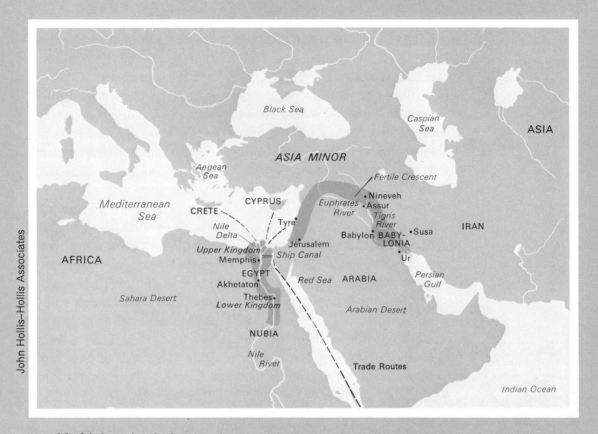

would think twice before trying to take your place. It would
be quite easy to keep your throne then. It would also be easy
to get your own way in everything.

Because of this belief that they were gods, the pharaohs
found it very easy to get their own way, especially in the Old
Kingdom. They believed, just as their people did, that they
had the *divine right of kings* to do whatever they wished.
They believed they had a right to give orders of any kind
because they were gods. Of course, because they were really
human, these pharaohs sometimes made mistakes or sometimes
were too hard on the people. But no one complained about
any mistreatment, for if he had the pharaoh might have ordered
him to be killed, or he might have seen to it that the person
did not have any land or any house or any food, which would
be just as bad as being killed. The pharaoh owned everything
in the country, including all the land. His people worked the
land and gave a large share of their crops to the pharaoh.
His subjects also served in the army and built canals and buildings. Everyone had to depend on the pharaoh for everything
he needed. It paid to obey him, no matter what. The pharaoh
had what we call an absolute monarchy. That means that he

above: Egypt and
the Ancient
Near East

43

was a monarch, or king, who had complete and total power. Many later kings had absolute monarchies and ruled by what we have called the divine rights of kings, just as the pharaohs did. But not many of them were thought to be gods.

Since the pharaoh was only one man, he himself could not give all orders. He had to have help throughout the empire. So his *local officials* found out from him what he wanted done each day and then told the people. The pharaoh might want certain crops planted, a building put up, or some stone cut. He would tell his officials about it and they would give his orders to the people who did the work. There was no problem about getting people to do the work, because the pharaoh had ordered it. These officials all had different jobs. Some were judges, who followed a set of laws that has since been lost; some were priests; and some were managers of work projects. There were so many of these officials that the pharaoh could not speak to all of them directly. So he had *chief officials* who did that. These men lived at the palace. It became a very complicated setup, but it did work out. Hundreds of men kept careful records of all government business. In this way the pharaoh got what he wanted. Other people, like the chief officials, became very important too.

The pharaoh and the important people under him had more material things than the other people had. They were rich and had more than they needed just to live. So they spent much time and money in preparing for the best life possible after they had died. To keep their bodies from crumbling and to make a place for the things they wanted to take with them to the next life, they built tombs. Very early in the Egyptian civilization, these tombs were made of sun-baked brick. Later, when the Egyptians learned how to cut stone with their copper tools, they began to use blocks of stone for their tombs. This was the first type of stone building ever found.

Finally, the Egyptians began to make their tombs in the form of pyramids (peer'ah-midz). Some of these pyramids are still standing. The pharaohs made so many wonderful pyramids between 2700 B.C. and 2200 B.C. that this time is called the Age of Pyramids. The most magnificent of the pyramids, of course, were tombs for the pharaohs. And the most wonderful one of all was the tomb of a pharaoh we called Cheops (kee'ahps). You might sometime hear him called Khufu (koo'foo), which is his name in Egyptian, but Cheops and Khufu are the same man. His magnificent tomb—the Pyramid of Cheops—was found at Gizeh. It was built about 2900 B.C.

opposite: Stone head of an Egyptian king

left top: Notice how small the man appears in this close-up view of the pyramid of Cheops

left bottom: The pyramids of Gizeh

All pyramids are made of solid limestone. The Egyptians used limestone because they had a lot of it in their country. To build a pyramid, the Egyptians cut the limestone into huge blocks that sometimes weighed two and one-half tons. Since one ton weighs 2000 pounds, that means that one of these limestone blocks could weigh 5000 pounds. After the blocks were cut, they had to be taken to the place where the pyramid was to be built. Then they had to be put together to make the building.

The Pyramid of Cheops is such an amazing structure that it is called one of the *Seven Wonders of the World*. It is 450 feet high—more than a hundred times taller than you are. How do you suppose the Egyptians were able to get a block of stone that weighed 5000 pounds up that high without having modern machinery to help them? Historians think they used manpower to pull the blocks on giant sledges to the building site. Then the blocks were pulled up earth ramps and eased into position. And, of course, they did not put just one of these blocks in place. In the Pyramid of Cheops alone, they used 2,300,000 of these unbelievably heavy blocks. It was a solid mass of stone. Herodotus (heh-rahd'uh-tuss), an ancient historian, wrote that it took 100,000 men twenty years to build this pyramid.

Pyramids took so long to complete that some pharaohs gave orders to have the work on their pyramids started just as soon as they became ruler, just to make sure that everything would be finished by the time they died!

At just about the same time the pyramids were being built, the Stonehenge people also were making huge stone structures. These people had moved to England and Scandinavia—far away from Egypt. We know very little about them, but we have found the remains of some of the construction. What we have found, particularly in England, shows us that they knew how to move huge stones into a circle and to put other stones on top of them—stones that were much too heavy for a man to lift. What these constructions were used for is not certain.

Stonehenge,
England

Some people today think they formed a giant calendar based on astronomical events. Others think the constructions were used for some kind of religious rites.

The pyramids, you remember, were solid. A thing that is solid has no hollow spaces in it. That was the way the pyramid was made except that in the center of the lower part there was one open space. This was the room in which the body of the pharaoh was placed. Here also were the furniture, the statues, and the other things that he wanted to take with him into the next life.

The Egyptians expected to be resurrected (rehz-uhr-rekt'ed) after they died; that is, they expected to come to life again in the same body they had when they were alive. They expected this because that is what they believed had happened to the god Osiris (oh-sye'rihs).

The Egyptians, you remember, believed in spirits that were like things that they found in the world around them. But these spirits that the Egyptians called gods were also like men. They had life stories just as people do.

Osiris, one of the most important ancient Egyptian gods

Although there were many gods, two of the most important ones were Ra and Osiris. Ra was the sun-god. He was very powerful because he was like the sun. Osiris was the river-god. He was like the Nile that renewed the country of Egypt every year with its flood. Osiris, the god of the Nile, was said to have been resurrected.

The story was told that Osiris had been killed by the god of evil, named Set. After killing Osiris, the story said, Set cut up his body and put the pieces in different parts of Egypt. This made Isis (eye'sihs), the wife of Osiris, very sad. She went all over Egypt to find the parts of the body of her husband. When she had found all of the parts, she put them together again and brought Osiris back to life.

After this happened to Osiris, he became the god of death. His job was to judge the people who died and decide whether they should be punished or rewarded for the kind of lives they had led. The Egyptians believed that it was very important to keep on the good side of Osiris because they wanted to be rewarded after they died.

It is important to know that the Egyptians believed this story, because it tells us much about them. As the story grew older, another part was added to it. The wicked Set was punished by another god named Horus (ho'russ) who was the falcon-god and the brother of Osiris. Horus killed Set for what he had done to Osiris.

This part of the story is important because it shows us that the Egyptians liked the idea of good winning out over bad. Many people liked this idea, just as we do today. But such ideas were not always important to people, or even thought of. Such an idea is an attitude toward life. People's attitude toward life makes them act in certain ways. Attitudes toward life can change but it takes a long time. In the Old Kingdom, the people's attitude toward life was based on their belief that the pharaoh was a god. People did not question him. No one else had rights at all. This attitude, however, was to change in later years.

Egypt—the Middle Kingdom

Peace and co-operation among the people went on in the Old Kingdom—the Age of the Pyramids—for many centuries. Since one century is one hundred years, many centuries is a very long time indeed. The land of Egypt became very rich during this time and there was much more than enough of everything for the pharaoh and his people.

As we said earlier, the government was complicated and the officials who helped the pharaoh rule were divided into classes. Some were *priests*, who were particularly close to the pharaoh because they knew about the gods and the gods, of course, were very important to the pharaohs. The priests conducted all religious services, as you would expect; but they did something else—something that might be a little surprising—they were the doctors of the time, the "healers." Another class was the class of *nobles*. These people were very important, as important as the priests were. The nobles knew about government and made sure that the work that had to be done in the country was done. In return for their services to the pharaoh they received favors. Both the priests and nobles made their jobs hereditary—that means that when a priest or noble died his job was passed on to his son.

As time passed the nobles became very rich and powerful. The pharaohs had given them many things, especially large amounts of land. They were left to rule their own sections of the country. The nobles did not do very much work themselves; like the pharaoh, they had people to do that for them. The people who did the work were divided into classes, or groups, too. People who made things like pottery and glass vases were called *artisans*. They were free men. People who worked the land were called *farmers*. They gave a large part of their crop to pay taxes. Most of the people in Egypt were farmers, who worked the land owned by the pharaoh, the priests, or the nobles. They were the lowest class except for *slaves*. But slaves did not count in Egypt. The next highest class were the artisans. The highest class were the nobles and the priests. Of course, the pharaoh was in a class all by himself.

The Metropolitan Museum of Art, Rogers Fund, 1916, and contribution from Henry Walters.

Copy of original in Egypt. The Metropolitan Museum of Art, Rogers Fund, 1916, with a contribution from Henry Walters.

The Metropolitan Museum of Art. Museum Excavations, 1919-1920; supplemented by contribution of Edward S. Harkness and Rogers Fund, 1920.

The Metropolitan Museum of Art, Gift of Edward S. Harkness, 1917.

clockwise from above:

A model of an Egyptian traveling boat

Egyptian toilet articles—a mirror (a silver disk), two razors, and two honestones

A reproduction of an Egyptian crown and hair ornaments

Egyptian figure of a hippopotamus

Egyptian fishing boat, harpooning fish

The Metropolitan Museum of Art, Museum Excavations, 1919-1920, supplemented by contribution of Edward Harkness and Rogers Fund, 1920.

About 2200 B.C. the nobles got some strange ideas. At least these ideas were strange for people living in ancient Egypt. They began to realize that because of their land and the people they controlled they were nearly as rich and powerful as their pharaoh. They were so important that they did not have to do everything the pharaoh told them to do; he couldn't force them to obey him.

The nobles began to disobey the pharoah. In fact, for 150 years, they were trouble to the pharaoh. The time during which the pharaoh had so much trouble with the nobles is called the "Age of Nobles."

The pharaohs finally got back from the nobles the power they had lost and everybody behaved again as they used to. The pharaoh was again the most powerful one and no one disobeyed him.

During the Age of Nobles, the Egyptians began to take an interest in what was going on outside their own country, and they also moved the capital from a place called Memphis (mehm'fihss) to another place called Thebes (theebz). The capital of any country is the main city where the leader works. Rome is the capital of Italy; London is the capital of England. Memphis was the capital of Egypt during the Old Kingdom. Thebes was the capital of Egypt during the Middle Kingdom.

below left: Egyptian sea-going vessel of 1480 B.C. built by August F. Crabtree

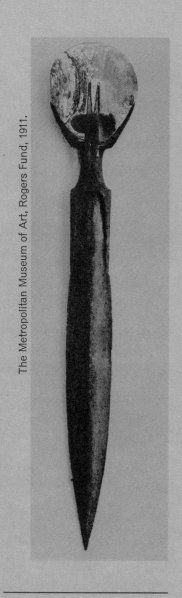

Egyptian bronze dagger

These two capitals were very different from one another. The main difference was that Thebes was a big city. Eygptians in the days of the Middle Kingdom were of two kinds. Some were *rural* people, which means they were people who lived in farming communities or small towns. Others were *urban* people, which means they were people who lived in a big city.

One of the pharaohs in Thebes decided to make his kingdom bigger. He took in land farther south, all the way to Nubia (noo'bee-ah). Nubia was a land of people who had very dark skins. The pharaoh put up a sign at the border of their land that told them not to come into his kingdom.

Other pharaohs paid more attention to the water supply than they did to acquiring more land. One of them built dams and a big stone reservoir (rehz'uhr-vwahr). A reservoir is something that holds water. This reservoir was huge, and was used to hold some of the flood water from the Nile. The pharaoh needed to keep some of the flood water because sometimes the Nile did not flood enough to make the land good for farming. When this happened, the pharaoh could take the water from the reservoir for the land. This pharaoh thought ahead.

The Egyptians at this time also did a lot of trading with other people. They were customers of the Phoenicians. They got wood from them to make coffins for the dead and also to make ships. Their ships sailed to the islands of the Mediterranean, perhaps even reaching Crete. Egypt did not have very many trees, so the Egyptians had to get wood from other places. The Phoenicians had many cedar trees that they traded. The Egyptians made a canal that ran from the Nile to the Red Sea so they could sail ships between the two places to make trading easier.

Even though the Egyptians did not want the Nubians to come into their land to live as settlers, they did want the people as slaves. Many times, groups of Egyptians went into that land to capture slaves. They also brought back gold and ivory and other things from Nubia.

Everything was going very well for the Egyptians until 1800 B.C. when the Hyksos took over. That ended the days of the Middle Kingdom.

This was the first time in a very long time that Egypt had been invaded. The Hyksos ruled parts of Egypt for 200 years. They had a well-organized, well-equipped army with horses and chariots, but they added nothing to Egyptian culture. Finally, in 1600 B.C., they were driven out of the country.

Egypt — the New Kingdom

When the Egyptians again gained control of their own country, they had the horse, the chariot, and the scimitar. They now had an army and a navy, and led by pharaohs from Thebes, they could make war on other people just as the Hyksos had made war on them. They began to go out of their own country and conquer other people and other nations. The New Kingdom became an empire of a kind, and that period is known as the "Age of Empire." An empire is a group of people or countries ruled by one powerful nation.

Thutmose III (thoot'moh'seh) was a great pharaoh at the beginning of the empire. He ruled for fifty years, from about 1500 B.C. Thutmose III was a great general who fought for twenty years to defeat Syria and Palestine. Pictures of this great pharaoh are found adorning the walls of the temple at Karnak and monuments called *obelisks*.

Whenever the Egyptians had defeated a smaller nation, they made these people pay *tribute*. Tribute may be money or other valuable things that a big and powerful person or country forces smaller people or countries to give them. In return for the tribute, the powerful country promises not to hurt the smaller, less powerful one. The Egyptians did one other thing to insure the loyalty and obedience of the nations they conquered. They took the son of the local ruler to the palace in Thebes. The father was left to carry out their orders. If this man did not do as he was told to, he knew the Egyptians might harm his son.

At this time, when Egypt was the most powerful country, a pharaoh named Rameses II (ram'seez) ruled. He was a very powerful man who had a very big army. Another people called the Hittites (hit'ites) were also powerful at that time and Rameses II wanted to conquer them.

Soon there was a long and terrible war between the Egyptians and the Hittites. This war lasted for twenty-five years. The end of the war was different from the end of the Egyptian wars during the days of the New Kingdom. Both sides really lost; the Egyptians and the Hittites were both weakened. Egypt never again was a strong and powerful country. Egypt, in time, was weakened even more by invasions of other countries, including new enemies who came from the north.

Before the war with the Hittites, and long before Rameses II was pharaoh, life in the New Kingdom had advanced in many ways and things had changed for many reasons. Of course, the pharaoh was still the ruler and he still told everybody what to do. The priests and nobles were the second most powerful people in Egypt and some traders and artisans had some power, too. The traders and artisans became the *middle class*. That means they were between the higher class of the priests and nobles, and the lower class of the farmers and other workers.

Egypt was very rich and the pharaoh, the priests, and the nobles had servants and slaves to wait on them; they wore beautiful clothes and had nice furniture, beautiful jewelry, and many other things. Life for them was very easy. The people of the middle class had some of these things but not nearly as much as the nobles and priests had. But the rest of the people had very little. They worked very hard and lived in little huts that were not at all like the beautiful houses of the more important people.

The great buildings that the Egyptians of the New Kingdom made were temples to their gods. They had stopped building pyramids before the New Kingdom began, during the Age of Nobles. During that time, people had begun to break into the pyramids and steal the things they found there. So the pharaohs and nobles began to build their tombs in tunnels. They had their workers dig these tunnels deep into the stone in their land so that the tombs would be hidden.

opposite top: Egyptian Empire at its height

opposite bottom: Reconstruction of the Temple of Queen Hat-shepsut in Thebes

EUROPE

ITALY   MACEDONIA   *Black Sea*

THRACE

PHRYGIA   *Iron Region*   *Caspian Sea*   ASIA

GREECE   LYDIA   *ASIA MINOR*

Aegean Sea   Sardis•   *Hittites*   ARMENIA

Fertile Crescent

ASSYRIA   •Nineveh

Mediterranean Sea   CRETE   CYPRUS   SYRIA   *Euphrates River*   •Assur

Tyre•   *Tigris River*

Babylon•BABY-   •Susa

Jerusalem•   LONIA   PERSIA

AFRICA   Memphis•   *Nile River*   Ur•

EGYPT   ARABIA

Akhetaton•   *Persian Gulf*

Sahara Desert   Thebes•   *Red Sea*

Arabian Desert

Indian Ocean

These tombs were so well hidden that people looking for them in modern times have had a very hard time finding them. But they did find an important one in 1922. It was the tomb of Tutankhamen (toot-ank-ah′ men), the son-in-law of Ikhnaton. Some people today call him "King Tut" for short. He had been pharaoh from about 1360 B.C. to 1350 B.C.—more than three thousand years ago. We found out a lot about life in the New Kingdom from that tomb in the Valley of the Kings near Luxor. Everything in the tomb was very grand. There were beautiful clothes and vases and jewels. There were golden beds, chariots, and garlands of flowers. And there was an unbelievably beautiful throne covered with gold, silver, and jewels.

The body of the young pharaoh was enclosed in three coffins, one inside the other. Each was decorated beautifully. The last was made of gold. It is shaped like a man and painted to look like Tutankhamen, who was only about eighteen years old when he died.

Tutankhamen had married the daughter of one of the most interesting pharaohs of all times. This interesting pharaoh was first named Amenhotep IV (ah-men-hoe′tehp). He began to rule in 1375 B.C. and he had the same power that all the other pharaohs had had. He was thought to be a god related to Ra, the sun-god.

Amenhotep had very new ideas about religion. He did not believe there were many gods as the other Egyptians thought. He believed that there was only one god, the sun-god. He called this one god Aton (ah′ton). To honor that god, Amenhotep changed his name to Ikhnaton (ik-nah′ton). The last part of the name "Ikhnaton" is the same as the name of the one god, Aton.

Ikhnaton fought with the priests of the old religion. He moved away from Thebes and had all the old temples to the gods closed down and ordered everyone to worship only Aton. Everybody did what he told them. But when this pharaoh died in about 1358 B.C. everybody went back to the old gods again and Aton was forgotten.

We are very much interested in Amenhotep's idea of religion because it is so much like the religions of Western civilization that came very much later. Amenhotep seems to have been very much ahead of his time in what he thought about religion. But the Hebrew people were the ones who gave the idea of one god, or *monotheism*, to the Western world, and that was much later.

The Sumerians and Akkadians

Egypt was not the only country that was making advances after the Copper Age, although it was the first one to do many things that civilizations do. To the east of Egypt there was another group of very intelligent people. They were the Sumerians (soo-meer'ee-unz), who lived in the land between the Tigris and the Euphrates rivers. In about 3500 B.C. they had moved down from the mountains to the Plain of Shinar and drained the marshes around the head of the Persian Gulf. This land was called Mesopotamia, but a part of it came to be called Sumer after them.

The Sumerians were as smart as the Egyptians and had learned the same things that the Egyptians had learned. They knew how to cultivate barley and wheat and they kept cattle, oxen, and donkeys to help them. They also knew how to write, how to make pottery, and how to work metal. They knew how to keep track of time, and even today we use their method of dividing minutes and hours into units of 60.

Like the Egyptians, the Sumerians believed in many gods and they believed that their gods would let them know what was the best thing for them to do. They built temples to their gods just as the Egyptians did, but the Sumerian temples were different from those the Egyptians had built.

The Sumerian people built their temples on hills, or mounds, in the shape of a pyramid. Steps led up to the top where next to the low temple building there was a very tall tower where the god was supposed to live. These mounds made of earth and the temples and towers on top of them, were called *ziggurats* (zig'oo-rats). They were always made in the same form. One of the tallest of these towers was the Tower of Babel.

The Sumerians did not believe in life after death as the Egyptians did, and therefore did not prepare for such a life. But they were very much interested in what their gods had to say to them during their lifetime. They would go to their priests and ask them to find out what the gods wanted them to do. The priests would sacrifice sheep and look at the livers of the animals because they thought that was the way to see what the gods wanted. Because the priest was supposedly the gods' representative, he was given much power. Only he

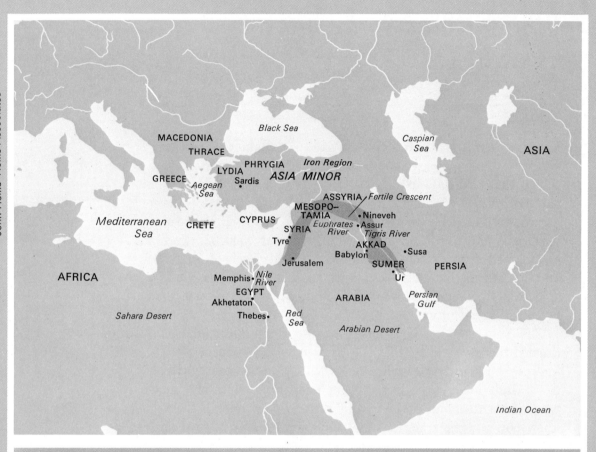

CUNEIFORM WRITING

ORIGINAL PICTOGRAPH	PICTOGRAPH IN POSITION OF LATER CUNEIFORM	EARLY BABYLONIAN	ASSYRIAN	ORIGINAL OR DERIVED MEANING
				OX
				SUN DAY
				GRAIN

(AFTER POEBEL)

could know what the gods wanted. So the priests gave commands. They were in fact *priest-kings* who ruled sections of the land. These sections were *city-kingdoms*. The priests were aided in their rule by the nobles of the city, who were wealthy and important.

When the Sumerians first began to write, they used pictures like the ones the Egyptians used. But later on, they discovered a better way to write on their clay tablets. You see, they did not have paper as the Egyptians had, and making pictures on clay was very difficult. It is, however, easy to make marks on soft clay with an instrument shaped like a wedge. The Sumerians developed such an instrument and with it they made wedge-shaped marks (triangular) on clay tablets. This kind of writing is called cuneiform (cue-nee'ih-form). These tablets have survived and tell us a lot about the people who wrote them.

The Sumerians did not build with big stone blocks as the Egyptians had done, for they had no stone in their land. They built with bricks made from mud. There was plenty of mud because their land was not dry the way Egypt was. In fact there are legends of fantastic floods in Mesopotamia during those days. Evidence has been discovered of one flood that covered the land with twenty-five feet of water! Now, however, it is very dry.

The Sumerians figured out something very clever to do with the mud bricks they made. They discovered how to make arches because they figured out the principle of the keystone, which held the bricks of the rounded arch in place. The Egyptians did not know how to make arches, and Egyptians doorways are square.

Since these people were very smart and since they lived in a land that was very easy to cultivate for food, you would think they would have gone ahead of the Egyptians in making a civilization. But they did not. And for a very important reason.

The land the Sumerians lived in had no natural protection from enemies. In Egypt there was desert on two sides of the Nile and the Mediterranean Sea on a third side. Boats could not go all the way down the Nile because the river was very rough in some places. But Mesopotamia was open everywhere. Anyone could walk right in.

Besides that, the Sumerian cities were not united. And they were always fighting with one another. The Sumerians could not really fight successfully against outside enemies when they were fighting wars against one another. And as if these things were not enough, a natural disaster had a terrible effect on the country.

opposite top: The lands of Sumer and Akkad

opposite bottom: Development of cuneiform writing

The first problem, the fact that the land of the Sumerians had no natural defenses, let many people from the desert areas move into it. Most of these people were Semites, people from one of three families we mentioned earlier. Most of them were desert people who wandered from place to place. In a steady but gradual flow the Semite people moved in with the Sumerians. A large group called the Akkadians (ah-kay'dee-unz) decided to form their own country—Akkad—in the area where the two rivers are closest to each other. They moved to the land right next door to the Sumerians. When they first came to that land, the Akkadians did not know very much about civilization. But they were very smart and soon learned from the Sumerians. They settled the land and learned the Sumerian cuneiform writing and used it to write their own language.

Just about the time the Akkadians had built up their land there was a huge flood that completely covered all the land of the Akkadians and the Sumerians. This was the flood that is written about in the Bible.

Even when the water finally went away, things were in a mess. Everywhere the water had been there was a giant layer of mud. The mud was seven feet deep. Can you imagine how things must have looked?

Even this did not discourage anyone, however, and more and more people came to the land of the Akkadians. Soon it was bigger than the land of the Sumerians. But the Sumerians were stronger and had well-made weapons. They could defend themselves from attack. And, finally, they became united. The head man of the city of Ur told the Sumerians that the gods wanted the cities to unite, and this city became the head of all of the Sumerian cities.

The unity and strength did not last long, however. In Akkadia, a man named Sargon (sar'gon) saw to that. He made war on the Sumerians in about 2500 B.C. When he won, he made everybody pay tribute to him.

Sargon established one of the first important Semitic kingdoms. Sargon's empire didn't last very long—about a century. The empire then went to pieces. Perhaps it fell as a result of attacks on the borders from outside barbarian tribes and from rebellions of the people within the empire.

For a short time before 2000 B.C., the Sumerian city of Ur again appears to have become strong. This was the last period of Sumerian independence. Power shifted constantly after this brief period. New invaders came and the Sumerians soon were absorbed completely by the Semites.

Sumerian battle scene

The god Shamash gives the law to Hammurabi

Mesopotamia's Golden Age

One of the cities of the Akkadians on the Euphrates River was to become very important. It was named Babylon. The Semitic tribe known as the Amorites settled there in about 2050 B.C. The city grew and grew until about 1900 B.C. when a ruler named Hammurabi (hahm-oo-rah'bee) conquered the area of Mesopotamia. Under Hammurabi, Mesopotamia was to have a "Golden Age," when things were very good for the people. So important was Hammurabi's influence that the Plain of Shinar, first settled by the Sumerians, now became called Babylonia.

Why was Hammurabi so important? Well, most kings like to talk about their conquests and how strong they are, but Hammurabi wanted to do nice things for the people. He saw to it that everyone was well fed and that the farms had enough water and that the houses were good. He ruled by the "divine right of kings," of course. That means, you remember, that he believed he was the ruler because the gods wanted him to be the ruler. But he also thought that it was more important for him to do things for the people than it was for the people to do things for him. That was a very different way for a king to act in those days.

He did something else that was strange and different for those days too. He had his scribes write down a code of laws and set it up for all to see. Because he represented the gods the people now knew exactly what the gods wanted. That may not sound strange to you, but in the days of Hammurabi and for all the time before that, no one really knew what the law was.

If people had a problem, they took it to the priests or the judges and these men told them what the law or what the gods thought about things. The people could never tell in advance about such things. In Babylonia they could read the law and could check up on the judges if they wanted to. The laws that Hammurabi made up were not easy laws. In fact, they were very hard, without mercy. They were based on the idea of "an eye for an eye and a tooth for a tooth." Maybe you have heard of that rule. If a man killed another man's son, for example, then his son would be killed. If someone

stole something, then he would have to pay back three times as much as he stole.

Even though the law was harsh, it was better than what the people had had. Hammurabi's Code of Laws answered questions for the people. It told the people what to do about their property, their land and houses, trade and commerce, marriage, family, agriculture, slaves, wages, and other things that were important in daily life.

It is hard to know just how many things the Babylonians discovered for themselves and how many things they learned from the Sumerians. However they got their knowledge, we have benefited from much of it. For one thing they seemed to know a lot about astronomy, the science of the stars and planets and other things in space. The knowledge they passed on is very important to us, for if we did not understand astronomy, we would not have even calendars and clocks.

The Babylonians had a calendar that was something like the one we use today. It was very different from what the

Egyptians used. The Babylonian calendar was based on the way the moon travels. You know that the moon travels around the earth in a path that is called an orbit. It takes the moon twenty-eight and one-half days to go around the earth once. The Babylonians used this period of time as their month. So every month in the Babylonian calendar had twenty-eight and one-half days.

All the time the moon is traveling around the earth in the path of its orbit, the earth is traveling around the sun in a path of its own. The earth's path is also called an orbit. It takes the earth 365 days to travel around the sun once more. The Babylonians made 365 days the length of one year, which is what we do today.

The Babylonian months were shorter than our months and so they had to have thirteen of them to fit into one year. Their days were like ours, however, There were twenty-four hours in a day and there were sixty minutes in an hour.

The Babylonians knew about some of the stars and about five of the planets. They also divided the circle into 360 degrees just as we do. But their number system was different from ours. Our number system is based on ten. Their number system was based on sixty.

The Babylonians, like the Sumerians before them, had many gods. They were very superstitious and used charms and spells to ward off evil spirits. They believed that spirits could cause failure of their harvests, sickness, and even death. They did not have any real belief in a life after death.

Business was so important to the Babylonians that they carried it on everywhere, even in the temples. Caravans traveled the countryside carrying goods. There was no coined money, and business was carried on by a process called *barter*. That means that they exchanged things, traded.

The "Golden Age" came to an end with the renewed flood of barbarian horsemen who raided the plains. One tribe, the Hittites, came and plundered and destroyed the land, but they did not stay. Another tribe, the Kassites, stayed. About 1250 B.C. they set up a loose rule over Mesopotamia. It was under their rule that Babylonia was governed for 600 years.

(text continued on page 80)

opposite: Skeleton of a Woolly Mammoth

above: Cavemen use rocks, torches, and primitive spears in their attempt to kill a Woolly Mammoth

overleaf: The Cavern of the Spy, once inhabited by Paleolithic man
International Visual Aids Center, Belgium

International Visual Aids Center, Belgium

above top: Stone tools from the Neolithic period

above: Polisher and polished axe, stone tools from the Neolithic period

right: Stone Age family making tools and weapons inside their cave dwelling

opposite above: The solid gold inner coffin of King Tutankhamen of Egypt, who ruled from about 1360 B.C. to 1350 B.C.

opposite below: Two Egyptian women weave on a horizontal loom

above: Egyptian sculptured figures—Pahotep and Nofret

An Egyptian
papyrus
with
hieroglyphics

A group of Phoenician traders unload their wares
on the shore near a Mediterranean town

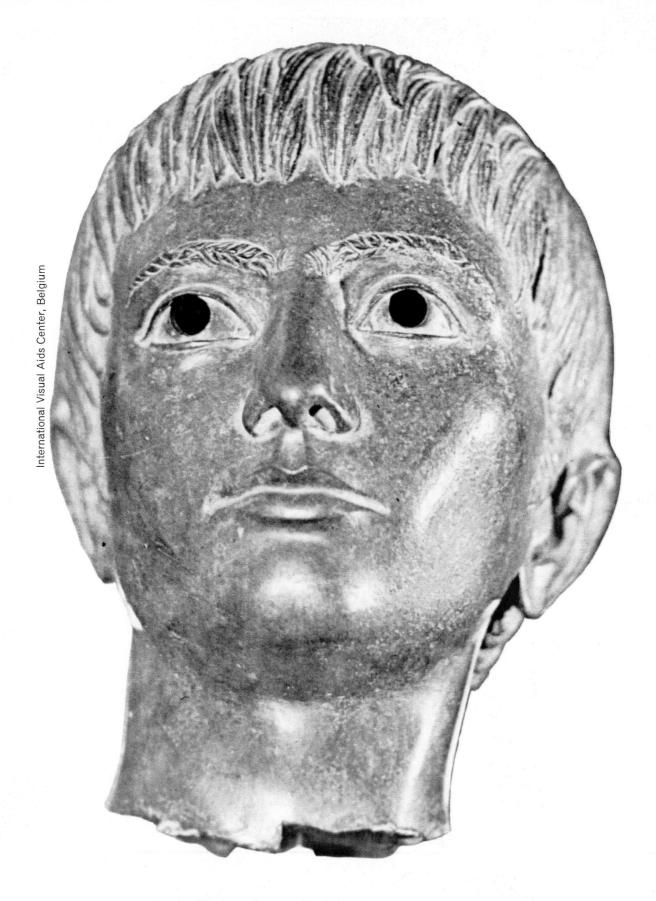

opposite: An Etruscan fresco of a flute player

above: An Etruscan bronze head of a young boy

(text continued from page 65)

About 200 miles north of Babylonia, in the upper valley of the Tigris, was another land and another people who were to become important. The land of Assyria (ah-seer'ee-ah) and the people in it had prospered in the valley of the Tigris River for many, many years. People lived there as far back as 7000 B.C. But they had not made important advances. In about 3000 B.C., Semites moved in. They were to make the land important and famous. These people were called Assyrians.

Notice how many important things happened about 3000 B.C. Just a little before that, in 3400 B.C., history began. That was when the Old Kingdom of Egypt was doing very well. And about 3500 B.C. the Sumerians moved into Mesopotamia. Now we are talking about another people who were starting a new civilization in about 3000 B.C. Many important things had certainly happened during the Copper Age. The people were doing much more than just learning to use copper.

The Assyrians had a head start because they were so close to Babylonia. They learned about writing and the calendar, about manufacturing and just about everything else from the Babylonians. You might think they would have had much the same kind of life the Babylonians had, but one thing made the Assyrians very different from their Babylonian neighbors. And it was to change the whole story of history.

That one thing that made the difference was the land itself. The Babylonians lived in a beautiful land that was not hard to cultivate, but the Assyrians did not have such good land. Theirs was harder to work. And besides, there often were raids by barbarians and the Assyrians were forced to spend much time in protecting themselves. Barbarians are people who are not civilized; that is, they do not know things that are common to those people they raid. Barbarians are ignorant and get what they want by taking it from others.

Barbarians lived very near the Assyrians and often made raids on Assyrian villages. The Assyrians learned to fight very hard to protect themselves, and fighting became a way of life for them. Their chief god was a war-god called Assur. Some Assyrians also worshipped the chief Babylonian god, Marduk, but Assur was the one the Assyrians made famous. His symbol was a disk with wings, a symbol that soon came to be feared by the people of other lands because it meant cruel and terrible war to them.

About 1250 B.C. a new king took the throne of Assyria and established a new dynasty. He and his sons and grandsons were to make the world a very different place from what it

The
Assyrian
Empire

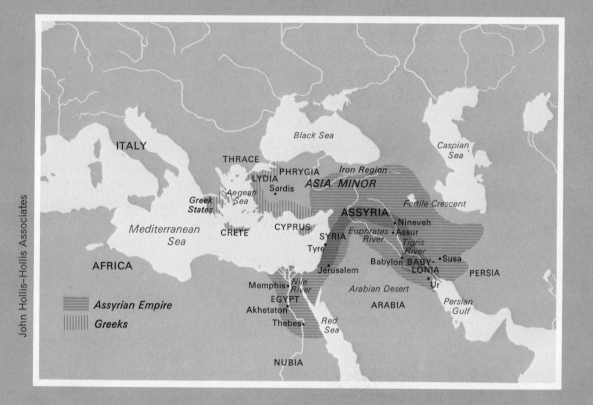

had been. The Golden Age of Babylonia had come to an end and a new influence, Assyrian, was to shape men's lives.

These Assyrian kings had in mind the conquest of the world about them. And they went about it in a very different way from what kings of other countries had done. Usually, when kings wanted to make raids or go to war, they called some of their people to follow them. When they finished their business the soldiers went back home.

But the Assyrian kings organized a *standing army*. A standing army is a group of soldiers who make the army their lifework. When there are wars, they fight. When there are no wars, they train for war. Almost all countries today have standing armies, but the Assyrians were the first people in the world to have one.

A country with a standing army is better able to go to war, either for conquest or to protect itself. The standing army is always trained, always ready. It does not have to take time to prepare for action.

The standing army of the Assyrians had excellent weapons. They were made of iron rather than bronze. The Assyrians had foot soldiers, chariots, and a cavalry. This was something new

above: The Assyrian Empire

to warfare. Cavalry are groups of soldiers mounted on horse-back. Some of the soldiers on foot were archers, who carried bows and arrows, and some were shield-bearing spearsmen. Both foot soldiers and the horse-drawn charioteers could fight the battles on the chosen field. But they were limited in their movement. The cavalry, however, could chase an enemy over difficult land. There was just no escape from the Assyrian army with all these advantages.

Nothing stopped the Assyrians. Even natural defenses like rivers did not stop them, for each Assyrian soldier had an animal skin that he could fill with air. He then could cross a river using the buoyant skin to hold him up. These skins were used in the same way water wings or life preservers would be used today. The Assyrians also were very good at attacking fortified towns. They used battering-rams, which were heavy tree trunks or pieces of machinery used to knock down the gates or walls of forts. If they could think of no other way to get into the fort of an enemy, they dug tunnels underneath the walls.

The first thing the Assyrian kings did when they had their huge army ready was to drive the barbarians far back from their own lands. Then they took over Babylonia. After this they went west and took over Syria, the country of the Hittites. All of this took several hundred years of almost constant fighting. During the eighth century the Assyrians had a king who was a very good general. He took the name Sargon, after the Semitic leader who had ruled more than 1800 years before. He called himself Sargon II, and ruled from 722 B.C. to 750 B.C.

Sargon II fought the Medes (meedz), who lived in the hills of Iran, and he even made war on the Egyptian pharaoh. He did this because the pharaoh was getting tribute from the Medes. Sargon II wanted the tribute for himself, and he got it. His successors—Sennacherib and Esarhaddon—also fought the Egyptians. Finally the Assyrians defeated the Egyptians. By 670 B.C. the Assyrian kingdom stretched across the Fertile Crescent and included Babylonia, Israel, Egypt, and Phoenicia.

All this time the Assyrians were doing more than just making raids on other people to show how strong they were and to collect tribute. They did collect tribute, of course, but they did something else, too—something that had never been done before. They established an empire.

How do people establish an empire? Well they manage to rule all of the territory they have taken. Before the Assyrians did it, kings had not really ruled other lands. Some had been

Bob Brunton–Hollis Associates

Assyrian foot soldier

strong enough to force the people to pay tribute. If the people did not pay tribute, the king who had won the war would return and punish them. But the Assyrians actually built forts in these faraway places and sent their own people to rule in them. These people, about sixty in all, were called *governors*. They reported directly to the Assyrian king. Royal messengers on horseback went back and forth constantly carrying letters and reports. They had a kind of mail service. That was new, too.

The Assyrians made all the people in their empire co-operate with one another. This spread civilization, because in order for the people to co-operate, there had to be a great exchange of information.

Although the Assyrians did keep their empire together and did grow very rich, the people they ruled hated them. The Assyrians had been very cruel in war and they were also cruel in peace. They were not like Hammurabi, who had wanted to make life better for his people. The Assyrians really did not care what happened to the people they had conquered. They cared only about the riches they could take from the lands they held.

By the time the empire was established, the Assyrians had a new city for the capital. It was named Nineveh (nihn'eh-vah). The Assyrian kings were very proud of Nineveh. The palaces they built show that the builders had further developed their skill. The arch, first seen in the simple homes of the Sumerians, appeared in Nineveh in a series of three—a triple arch— decorated with beautifully colored glazed bricks. Alabaster sculptures lined the walls of the palace buildings. Most of them show the accomplishments of the emperor. The pictures the Assyrians made of animals are more natural and show more life and emotion than the pictures they made of men. The people in their pictures often look stiff and unnatural.

The library of King Assurbanipal, who reigned from 668 B.C. to 626 B.C., was uncovered by an archaeologist in about 1845 (A.D.). It contained clay tablets of every type—religious, scientific, and literary. There were found more than 20,000 clay tablets in all. This was the first library of its kind known. The tablets are now in the British Museum.

King Sennacherib made certain there would be a water supply for the city of Nineveh. He built a series of huge water conductors, or conduits, and aqueducts that carried water for more than thirty miles from the mountains in the north.

The Assyrians had made Nineveh very beautiful with all the riches they had taken from the conquered people of their empire. It stretched for two and one-half miles along the Tigris

Assyrian horseman

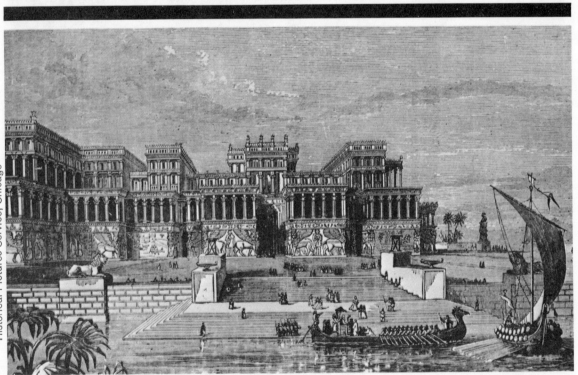

River. Soon Nineveh became a hated name to these conquered people.

The hatred of these people grew and grew. And the Assyrians themselves became weaker and weaker. There were invasions from outside the land and revolts of the people from within. Industries were destroyed and plundered during battles and the farmland was untilled because the farmers either left it or were killed during fighting. And the Assyrian army became weaker and weaker. The Assyrians had been at war for such a long time that many of their army had died and many of those people who had to rule the conquered people had become tired from the careful attention they had to pay to everything they held. The empire was really too large to be governed properly. When the Assyrian army began to grow too small because so many of the soldiers had been killed, the kings had to use mercenaries (muhr'seh-nair-eez), hired soldiers who fight for money. Mercenaries do not belong to the country that hires them, but are foreigners who do not feel loyalty to the king of the country they fight for. They are never such good soldiers as the native people. The Assyrians also forced their conquered subjects to serve in the army. These people, of course, didn't make very good soldiers, for they hated the rulers.

As the army grew weaker, barbarians invaded the territory of the empire. A desert tribe, the Chaldeans (chall-dee'unz), who had been settling around the Persian Gulf for hundreds of years, joined the Medes to fight the Assyrians. Then the Babylonians revolted and fought on the side of the Medes against the Assyrians. The Assyrians were defeated and their beautiful capital city of Nineveh was completely destroyed in 612 B.C. An Old Testament prophet tells of the glad shout that went up from the Caspian Sea to the Nile River when the subject nations heard of the downfall of their enemy. Only a few mounds are left today to show where the great city of Nineveh was. The Assyrian Empire had lasted from 750 B.C. to 612 B.C.

opposite top: A relief showing King Sennacherib's cavalry in the mountains

opposite bottom: An artist's interpretation of the royal palace at Nineveh

After the Assyrian Empire was destroyed, the desert tribe of Semites—the Chaldeans—took over most of it and it became the Chaldean Empire.

One of the most famous kings of the Chaldean Empire was Nebuchadnezzar II (nehb-uh-kad-nehz'uhr). He fought many wars and conquered other peoples. Some of the people he conquered were from the land of Egypt, some were from the land of Syria, and some were from the land of Phoenicia. He had a very hard time conquering the people of Jerusalem. When he finally did conquer them, he took many of them back to Babylonia with him and kept them there in terrible captivity. Nebuchadnezzar II was a very cruel man, but he was the greatest ruler of the Chaldean Empire, and he made Babylon the greatest city that had ever been seen.

The city of Babylon was perhaps the most famous city in ancient times. It was on the edge of the Euphrates River; part of the city was on one side and part was on the other. Archaeologists believe it was a city of great size, perhaps five square miles in area, and was surrounded by two massive defensive walls. One of these walls was so wide that two chariots could pass on it at the same time.

Eight gates led into this ancient city. Each one was dedicated to a favorite god. The Ishtar Gate led to a magnificent limestone road. This street crossed the city and ended at the sacred tower built to honor the god Marduk. The tower was built of many-colored bricks, and was later thought to be the Tower of Babel, but according to archaeologists the tower in Babylon was built at a later time, and was part of Nebuchadnezzar's city.

The most famous feature of the ancient civilization in this city was the Hanging Gardens. Some people think these were built by Nebuchadnezzar to please his wife. The lush green foliage reminded her of her homeland, Media. They were only a part of the royal palace, but they were very beautiful. The gardens were built on brick terraces and went in steps up to the very top of the palace. Gardens full of trees, flowers, and shrubs surrounded the royal court. Here the royal families could spend time in pleasant, cool places that were very different from their natural surroundings. A special system of buckets and chains made it possible to pull water up to the very highest terrace. From there it ran down to irrigate the

opposite top: Nebuchadnezzar, King of Babylon, conquers Jerusalem

opposite bottom: The Medean and Chaldean Empires

The destruction
of Babylon
by the Persians

lower levels. From this fantastic garden the king could overlook his splendid city.

The Chaldean Empire borrowed much from the great empires that preceded it. But in the study of astronomy they made very great advances on their own. The Chaldeans were among the first to keep regular records of astronomical events such as eclipses. They observed the skies and kept continuous records. Some of these records were kept for over three hundred years! Not only were they kept but they were used. About 500 B.C. the Chaldeans made tables that were used to calculate the length of a year. The tables were so accurate that they were only about twenty-seven minutes off.

The Chaldeans also used the heavens as their guide in religion. The five planets known then were Mercury, Venus, Mars, Jupiter, and Saturn. Like other Semitic peoples, the Chaldeans believed the heavens influenced men's destiny, so their gods were directly connected with these heavenly bodies—to which we must add the sun and moon—seven in all. So it is that their goddess of love, which in Chaldean was Ishtan, in Roman times became Venus, and their god Marduk became the Roman god Jupiter.

There were seven gods and seven days of the week. As the years passed and such ideas spread to Syria, it became the custom to worship a certain god on each particular day of the week. So it is that we have come to know certain days as Sunday, Monday, and Saturday. These days were named to honor the Sun, the moon, and the planet Saturn. Later on you will find out how the other days were named.

All during this time when the Chaldeans were making such great advances and Nebuchadnezzar was making the city of Babylon and his own palace so beautiful, people of the hill countries not so very far away—the Persians—were making a huge army. The Persians were Aryans, an Indo-European people who lived in the country that is now called Iran (ee-rahn'). In 539 B.C. they attacked and conquered the city of Babylon, which was completely destroyed. All of its wealth and wonder were ruined or removed from the scene. Today if you travel in this area there is nothing left but sculptures made of brick mixed with pitch. These stand as the sole symbols of Babylonia's magnificent past. The Persians were to become the most important people in all the land we have been talking about. They were to conquer all the people we have discussed and more besides.

The Traders and the Money Makers

Look closely at the map on page 96. The land below and to the right of Mesopotamia connects the land of Egypt with the land of Mesopotamia. Much of the land down at the bottom of the map is really desert, just sand. But the land nearer the Mediterranean Sea is very good farmland. Because the land was good people built villages and cities there.

These people lived in Syria (sihr'ee-ah), Asia Minor, Phoenicia (fih-nee'shuh), and Palestine (pal'ess-tine). Much of what happened to them happened because of their location. They lived in a land that people had to go through to get from Egypt to Mesopotamia and back again. People who had camels could go right through the desert, but this was a slow, hard way to go. Soldiers and traders liked to move fast and traveled through the land near the Mediterranean Sea.

Desert people called Amorites (am'oh-rites) first settled in Syria in about 2500 B.C. That was near the time of the Old Kingdom period in Egypt and when the country of Babylonia was being formed.

Because they were living in the path of the trade route, the Amorites themselves became traders. They learned about civilization from the travelers who passed through their land. They built cities that were independent of one another and never did learn how to work together to push out people who made war on them. The country had no natural defenses and the people were always being conquered and made to pay tribute. Remember how the Egyptians and the Assyrians conquered them?

The people who first lived in Asia Minor were the Hittites, whom we have talked about before. We saw how they captured

Babylonia. The history of the Hittites can be divided into two periods of time. The first one, the time of the *Old Kingdom,* began when the tribes of Hittites united under one king. The second period of time, the *Empire Period,* was when the Hittites were conquering other people and building an empire. This period lasted from about 1460 B.C. to 1220 B.C.

We are interested in the Hittites mainly because we are fairly sure that they started the Iron Age. They found huge amounts of iron in the hills of their land and learned how to get it out of the ground and use it to make iron weapons. They also began to trade it to people for other things.

The people who lived in Phoenicia, however, became the really important traders. The Phoenicians had very little land, but what they did have was right on the Mediterranean Sea. Since they also had large and beautiful cedar trees in their land, they could build big boats and learn to sail. They became explorers because they were always looking for new lands, and for people with whom they could trade. The Phoenicians originally had been a wandering desert people, but now they became a wandering sea people.

The Phoenicians became very smart businessmen. They soon discovered that they could do something more than just trade what they had for something they wanted. They found that they could make trades for other people, too. They became "middlemen," the first big suppliers of goods that they did not make themselves.

The Phoenicians moved around more than any other people. And besides trading and distributing goods, they also traded and spread knowledge everywhere they went. In this way they helped civilization grow in many parts of the ancient world.

The Phoenicians helped give us our alphabet by spreading knowledge. They needed to have a bookkeeping system for

Hittite sculpture

their business, and at first borrowed the Egyptian sound symbols to use for making the words they needed to keep their accounts. They soon made up their own alphabet. It was not like the alphabet we use. It looked different and had only twenty letters, all consonants, as in the Egyptian alphabet. While they were trading with the Greeks, the Phoenicians showed them the alphabet. The Greeks borrowed it and made one for themselves that was something like the Phoenician alphabet. Later, the Romans learned the alphabet from the Greeks. The Romans made some changes in that alphabet to make the Roman alphabet. The modern Roman alphabet is the one used today in western Europe and the Americas, it is nearly identical to the ancient Roman alphabet.

Palestine, at the western end of the fertile crescent, was first settled by people called Canaanites (kay'nun-ites). They had been nomads until about 3000 B.C. when they came to Palestine and settled there. This was not long before Menes ruled in the land of Egypt. The Canaanites learned how to farm and they learned about gods from some of the people they found in the land when they came there. As time passed, they learned about cuneiform writing and law from people in Mesopotamia. They learned about pottery and gold and silver and soldiers from people in Egypt.

Sometime about 1550 B.C. a group of nomadic shepherds of the Arabian Desert began to make raids on the land of the Canaanites. These people were the Hebrews.

The Hebrew people were to become very important to us. They were the ones who first came to believe in only one God. The Hebrews called their God *Yahweh*. The belief in one God is called *monotheism*, and this idea is still held by most people in the Western world today. The Hebrew people eventually established a religion called Judaism. The Christian religion had its roots in Judaism, so two of the great religions of the modern world came from these Hebrew people who settled in Palestine.

The history of the ancient Hebrew people comes to modern man through the Bible. The early Hebrew people wrote the Bible, which contains their history and also their ideas about what is good and what is bad. The Bible is one of the most important remaining sources of information and literature of the ancient world.

According to the Bible, Hebrew history began when a man named Abraham left Ur with his family, about the time when Hammurabi ruled Babylonia. They went into the desert, but could find no food, so they kept moving. Some of the descendents of Abraham went to the land of Goshen (go'shun), which is the name they used for Egypt. The Hebrews were taken as slaves and found life very difficult in Egypt. They wanted something better, but did nothing about it until their leader, Moses, led them out of Egypt to freedom. Moses told the people that God told him to lead them to the "Promised Land."

The Bible says that on their way to the "Promised Land" the people received the Ten Commandments from God. Finally the people reached the "Promised Land," which was Canaan, where the Canaanites lived. They settled near the towns and cities of the Canaanites, but for a long time they had no permanent homes but lived in tents just as they had when they were wandering shepherds. Some of the Hebrew people who had not gone to Egypt had already settled there.

By about 1000 B.C. the Hebrew people joined into a kingdom. Saul was the first king. He was a very good fighter and he developed an army. Saul lived in a tent when he was king, but David, his successor, took by force the old Canaanite fortress of Jerusalem for the kings' permanent strong defensive home and Jerusalem became his capital. Songs, or psalms, found in the Old Testament are believed to have been written by David, the second king of the Hebrews.

David's son, Solomon, reigned next. Solomon had come a long way from the simple tent home of Saul. Solomon liked luxury, and helped make Jerusalem a very lovely city. In it he built the beautiful Temple of Jerusalem. In order to pay for the expensive things he wanted for himself and his city, he demanded very heavy taxes. He taxed his people until they became very angry.

Soon after Solomon died some of the people from the northern part of the kingdom set up a kingdom of their own and called it Israel. The southern part became known as Judah. So it was that by about 930 B.C. the Hebrew kingdom was divided into two parts.

Israel, in the north, was very wealthy; there were towns and cities, markets and prosperous farms. Judah in the south, was very poor in comparison. The land was not as fertile and there were no large towns here. The only major city in Judah was Jerusalem. The people in the North were townspeople and those in the South were country folk.

The townspeople of Israel seemed not to keep their earlier beliefs about right and wrong. They began to forget that their

ITALY   MACEDONIA   *Black Sea*   *Caspian*
                                                             Sea
           THRACE
                         PHRYGIA   *Iron Region*
                 LYDIA   ASIA MINOR
      GREECE   Sardis•   ARMENIA
           Aegean   •Hittites
           Sea   ASSYRIA
Mediterranean   CRETE   CYPRUS   MESOPOTAMIA •Nineveh MEDEA
    Sea   *Euphrates* •Assur
                         SYRIA   *River*   *Tigris*
                         PHOENICIA   *River*
                   PALESTINE   Babylon• BABY- •Susa
                         •Jerusalem   LONIA   PERSIA
AFRICA   Memphis• *Nile*   •Ur
                         River
                   EGYPT   ARABIA   *Persian*
                   Akhetaton•   *Gulf*
Sahara Desert   Thebes• *Red*
                            Sea   *Arabian Desert*

religion had taught belief in one God and found it easier to believe in many gods, as did their neighbors.

The people of Judah, however, had kept many of their simple ways. They were not as far removed from the days when they had been poor wandering shepherds as were the Israelites. They continued to worship their God, and continued to be comforted by their belief in him.

The great Hebrew prophet Amos went into the North and tried to persuade the people of Israel to return to the simple ways and one god of their forefathers. He told them to trust in God and to be kind and just to their fellow man.

Amos had predicted that there would be danger to Israel from outside the country, and time proved him right. In 722 B.C. the Assyrians invaded and conquered Israel. They took away most of the people who had lived there, and Israel was completely wiped out.

The little kingdom of Judah, poor and alone, fought on. To the simple people of the time it appeared to be a conflict between the gods—the Assyrian god, Assur and their god, Yahweh. The people of Judah miraculously escaped destruction by Sennacherib's army in 701 B.C. This made them believe that their God was not just in Palestine, and the prophet Isaiah proclaimed that Yahweh was god of the whole world.

Though the Assyrians did not capture Judah, in 586 B.C. the Chaldean king Nebuchadnezzar II conquered the country, and the Hebrew people of Judah suffered as those of Israel had suffered earlier. The city of Jerusalem was destroyed and many of the people were taken to Babylonia as captives. Here the Hebrews were faced with the same question that seemed to keep returning; was their God with them in their exile or not? During their exile they came to feel that Yahweh was a father and ruled the world righteously and well. This belief was very helpful to them during this time and thereafter. So it was that the Hebrew people preserved their belief in one God for future generations.

opposite top: The Egyptians urge Moses to depart

opposite bottom: The Ancient Near East

97

Except for the Hittites and Medes, all the people we have discussed so far have been Semitic. Now we are going to see how the Indo-European peoples began to change history. As you may remember, the Persians were a group of Indo-Europeans who called themselves Aryan. They lived in a land that was quite far from Mesopotamia, on the other side of the Persian Gulf. It is now called Iran, which comes from the word Aryan.

These Indo-European people came to Iran before 1000 B.C. There were two groups, the Medes and the Persians. At first, the Medes who lived in the north part of the land ruled over the Persians, who lived in the south part.

In those days the land was very fertile. There was enough rain and the hills were green and the soil was rich. The very early settlers were farmers and herdsmen, but even though they farmed the land and raised animals for a living, they also had learned how to ride horses and shoot with bows and arrows.

During the days of the Assyrian Empire, these people paid tribute to the Assyrian kings. But the Medes, you remember, helped the Chaldeans defeat the Assyrians. This was part of the reason why the Assyrians lost their empire.

After the Medes helped defeat the Assyrian Empire, the Persians revolted against the Medes. The Persians won and became the rulers of the Medes. They seemed to be content to rule only these people until about 550 B.C. when a man named Cyrus (sye'russ) had an idea.

The Persian Empire

Cyrus was a Persian chief who decided to bring the Medes and the Persians together into a huge and powerful army so that he could conquer all of the ancient world. The first land he conquered was Lydia, a small kingdom in Asia Minor. The Lydians had been the first people to make coins for money. They made them from *electrum*, which is an alloy of gold and silver. Up until this time people who traded and did business had no money. They traded one thing for another or gave bars of valuable metal for goods they wanted. If the goods were less in value than the metal bar, they had to cut the metal into smaller pieces, which was very hard to do.

After he conquered the Lydians, Cyrus next conquered the whole Chaldean Empire and began to make plans for taking over Egypt as well. Before he could do this, however, he died.

That did not stop the Persians. The leader who came after Cyrus went right on to conquer all of Egypt. His name was Cambyses (kam-bye'seez). When he finished his part of the war, the Persians had conquered nearly all of the ancient world. And they did all this in only fifteen years. They were very good at fighting wars.

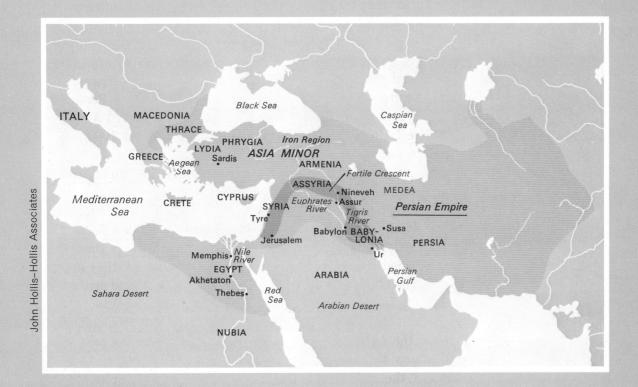

Until they had conquered all the land that made the great Persian Empire, the civilization of the Persians was behind that of many other lands. But these people learned very fast. The civilizations they conquered had many things to offer, and the Persians rapidly began using them. From the Babylonians they learned to write with cuneiform symbols. Also from the Babylonians, and from the Egyptians, they learned about beautiful buildings. Soon they made their own cities as beautiful as the cities in the conquered countries.

The Persians were good at government. They divided the whole empire into sections called satrapies (say'trah-peez). In each of these satrapies there were Persian officials who did the business of the empire. They collected tribute and acted as judges and did all the other things that government officials have to do.

They reported to the Persian leaders by messenger. This messenger service was better and faster than the one the Assyrians had had because the Persians had built good roads all through their empire.

The Persian kings also had troops in all parts of the empire, in case the people wanted to revolt. But the people did not revolt; they were content. The Persians were not cruel and hard on them as the Assyrians had been on the people they had conquered.

above: The Persian Empire at its height

The people could travel over the roads the Persians had built and do business with parts of the empire far away from their homes. They liked this. Also, the travel brought to the least civilized people the knowledge that the most civilized people had. The whole empire became more civilized and advanced faster. The whole area, which is called the Near East, became very highly civilized then.

The Persians greatly influenced the religious ideas that were developing at this time. Most of their new ideas came from a man named Zoroaster (zoe-roe-ass'tuhr), who lived about 1000 B.C. When he was a young man, Zoroaster had seven visions. During these visions he talked with a great god and his archangels. This god told him many, many things which later were written down in gold letters upon the hides of oxen. Although the original writings have been lost, most of the information once written here has been passed down in writings of other people. The total collection of material from Zoroaster and his disciples, or followers, is collected in a book called *Avesta*. This was the Persian Bible.

Zoroaster was told that there was one god above all other gods. This god made the whole world and the sun and stars and everything else in space. His name was Ahura Mazda (ah-hoo-raa maaz'daa). He created only things that were good; Ahura Mazda was the god of light and life.

But there was another god called Ahriman (ah-rih-man') who made everything that was bad. Ahriman was the god of darkness and death.

Zoroaster was told that although Ahura Mazda was greater and would always win, Ahriman would fight with him constantly. They did fight on and on, each trying to win out over the other. They fought for men's souls.

It was the job of the Persians to help the good god. They could do this by doing good deeds. But if they committed evil acts, this helped Ahriman. After death each man's soul was judged to see which god the man had served during his lifetime, for it was with that god that the man would spend eternity.

So the Persians believed that it was not just fate or chance that determined whether a man was rewarded or punished in the next world. This was quite different from other religious ideas which often said that man was not responsible for what happened to him after his death.

After the Persians had built their empire, they began to look around for other lands and other people to conquer.

Faraway Lands — India and China

Remember we said that men had gone over land bridges to all parts of the world thousands and thousands of years ago? What ever happened to them? We are not sure how most of these people lived very long ago, because we do not have any kind of records for many of them, but many, many years afterward we found their descendents still there. In two places, India and China, we also found important civilizations and some records. Just because we have not found records of very early civilizations in other places does not mean that there were none. There might have been. We just do not have any record of them. We are talking now only about things of which we have some kind of record.

We know that civilization began very early in India. People there began to live in villages when the Egyptians did. India is far to the south and far to the east of Iran. It belongs to the continent of Asia. Even before 1000 B.C. some people with fair skins moved into India. When they arrived, they found other people already living there. These first settlers had dark skins. They were called Dravidians (drah-vihd'ee-unz). The new people conquered the Dravidians and became rulers. They did not want to intermarry with the Dravidians and so they made up a caste system. In a caste system people are divided into groups by the color of their skin. In the Indian caste system the white-skinned people were the highest caste and the dark-skinned people were the lowest caste. The people in the highest caste were also divided into upper and middle class. The upper class people were nobles and priests. The middle class people were farmers. The people with dark skin who were in the lower part of the caste system were given jobs to do that were not so nice. They had a very hard time under this system. The system does not exist in India any more, but it did for a very, very long time.

We know about how the new people came into India because there is a book of poems the Indians have that tells us about it.

The *Rig Veda*, or the "sacred knowledge of praise," begins the recorded, or written, history of India. Although it tells

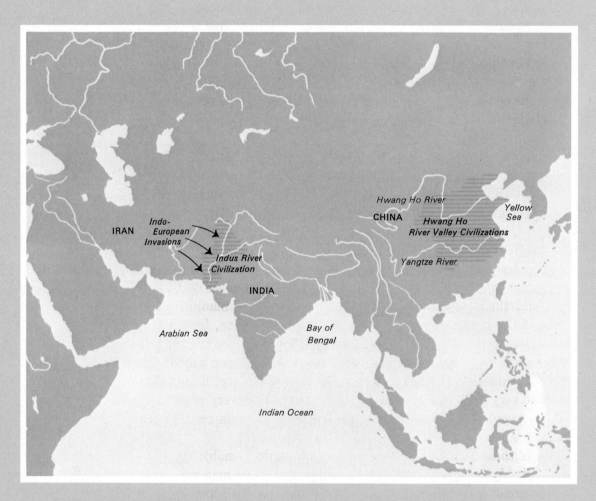

Map of Asia showing early civilizations in China and India

about the invasions of the Indo-Europeans, it was not written at this time. According to some authorities the oldest section of this book was written about 1200 B.C. Much of this section was handed down from generation to generation for hundreds of years before this.

During this time, 1200 B.C., the Egyptian Empire was already old and beginning to fail, the city of Babylon and the kingdom of Babylonia had fallen into the hands of the Kassite people and the kingdom of Assyria was on the rise.

The *Rig Veda* was written in the ancient language Sanskrit, which resembles ancient Greek, Latin, and Persian. This tells us much about the exchange of knowledge among the various peoples in this part of the world.

After the migration of the light-skinned people into India, life in the country resumed its normal pace. Most of the people lived in simple villages. Here a man's wealth and position were determined by the number of cattle he owned.

India was the scene of constant battles between lords and villages. Each tried to better the other and take over their property. During these battles the nobles or wealthy warriors rode in chariots and were protected with armor, shields, and swords. Often a priest rode with them, saying sacred prayers and muttering magic words to insure victory. The common soldier fought on foot.

The new people in India had brought with them their own gods and their own religion. This religion was Brahmanism. Some of the people, however, did not like this religion, for it did not have anything in it about making their minds and bodies pure. Some of the people who followed the religion went off by themselves to think about what man should be. They thought very long and very hard. And they lived a very poor life, as people who had nothing. They were what is called ascetics (ah-set′iks).

One of these ascetics was named Gautama (go-tah′mah). He was probably born about 500 B.C. He was a very good man and a very great teacher who taught that people should learn to have peace inside themselves. If they did good deeds and did not think about themselves too much he said they would not be sad and troubled no matter what happened. Many people listened to Gautama and believed what he said. They began to call him Buddha (boo′dah) and took his teachings as a new religion, Buddhism. Both Brahmanism and Buddhism today are great religions of the world. Many people believe in one or the other.

above: Close-up of a sculpture of Buddha

opposite: Chinese bronze ceremonial vessel; the cover is in the form of a human face with horns

above top: Chinese bronze tiger

above: Chinese bronze decorative animal

Chinese characters from
a ceremonial vessel

When the Persians went down into India they found a civilization that was different from theirs, but was very advanced.

The greatest very early civilization in India had been in the valley of the Indus River. Notice how very early civilizations seem to get started near great rivers. In Egypt, the Nile was the important river; other people did well near the Tigris and Euphrates rivers.

The people in the Indus Valley could farm and build houses and do many of the things that people far away were doing. They also developed beautiful art. Sometime after 3000 B.C., however, this wonderful civilization declined. Since it happened before the time of written records, we do not know just what it was that changed the life of these people who had been doing so well.

The Persians did not know it, but far, far to the east, in China, another civilization existed. It had had a very early beginning, too. People who lived there in the Stone Age had learned many things and had advanced in many ways, just as people who lived in the Near East had.

We do not know much about the very early times in China. But we do know that by the time written history begins in Egypt, a great civilization was developing around the Wei River (way) and Hwang Ho Valley (whang ho) in China. The people knew how to farm and how to make bronze. They were also very good craftsmen. About then they had their first kings, too.

Under the various dynasties the people developed great art, government, and manners. They had developed writing by about 600 B.C. and many great teachers and thinkers lived then.

One of the greatest teachers was a man named Confucius (kon-fyou'shus), who lived about the time Buddha lived. Confucius was a very wise man who told people how to live good lives, just as Buddha did. The things he taught were written down and his teachings became a religion.

The Persians and others would have been very much surprised to know about China and its civilization. But people from the West did not meet people from the East for a long, long time.

Civilizations in the Americas

It is thought that the Indians of North and South America came from Asia. Their remains show them to be more like the Asians than the Europeans or Africans. At the eastern edge of Russia, in Asia, the coastline is not far from Alaska in North America. The Indians probably crossed from Asia to Alaska using the Aleutian Islands as stopping places, or there may have been a land bridge they gradually moved across.

No definite date can be given to tell us when these people began to move into the western hemisphere, how long it took them to come, or when they did actually arrive, but it was a very, very long time ago.

The first settlers in the western hemisphere were probably Stone Age men who knew how to make their utensils from stone and probably knew how to make fire. They advanced according to their needs. If they settled in an area where there was plenty of game and good soil, they did not have to struggle to exist or invent new ways of living. If they lived in parts of the land where there were no rivers and not much rain, they had to learn how to irrigate their land and provide food for themselves.

The Indians who settled in the dry, high plains began farming and irrigating the land. Instead of raising the crops people raised in Europe and Asia, they raised corn. Corn was called *maize*, and grew well; in fact, it probably was a wild plant that the Indians found could be used for food.

Because the Indians had to farm and learn to irrigate their land, they were not wandering tribes. They had to settle down in one place, and so villages were developed. Men had to learn to live together and get along together, they had to build a civilization.

Clay was used for dishes, jugs, and pots and the women learned to weave cloth. Soon metals were discovered in rocks in the ground. They may have been discovered in much the same way they were discovered in Europe and Asia. Useful things were made with copper, but gold, silver, and tin were used for ornaments.

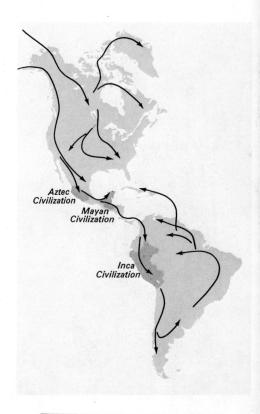

Possible migration routes of the Indians of the Americas

Three important civilizations developed in the western hemisphere; the Aztec in Mexico, the Mayan in Central America, and the Incan in Peru.

On the plateau where Mexico City now stands there was a tribe of civilized Indians called the Toltecs when the Aztecs arrived. When the Aztecs first viewed the settlement, it was a lake with islands scattered about. They conquered the Toltecs, built their dwellings on the islands, and built more artificial islands.

The Aztecs' city, almost a mile high, grew to have beautiful palaces and temples. The Aztecs had a calendar and a written language, and they knew how to mine the precious metals found in the area.

The Mayas in Central America settled in the lowlands. They cleared away the forests and had wonderful land for farming. They, too, had a system of writing and a calendar. They used a form of hieroglyphics and wrote on the bark of trees, on deerskin, or even on a kind of paper they made from a plant.

Unlike the Aztecs and the Incas, the Mayas were not a great civilization when the European settlers arrived in the New World. Because of civil war the Mayan civilization fell apart and few signs of their past advances were left to be seen.

The Incas settled in the highlands of Peru. They had a very orderly king who ruled his people well. Everyone had to work; some at farming, some at building, and some at mining. The men had to serve in the army, too. There were always other tribes to conquer, and a rich and powerful tribe or country must have an army to defend itself in case of attack.

The marvelous capital city of Cuzco still shows the building done by the Incas. The Temple of the Sun had gold walls on the inside, and a line of gold running around the outside wall. Another city of the Incas, Machu Picchu (mah'choo peek' choo), was not discovered until the twentieth century because it was so well hidden. It is called the "Lost City of the Incas."

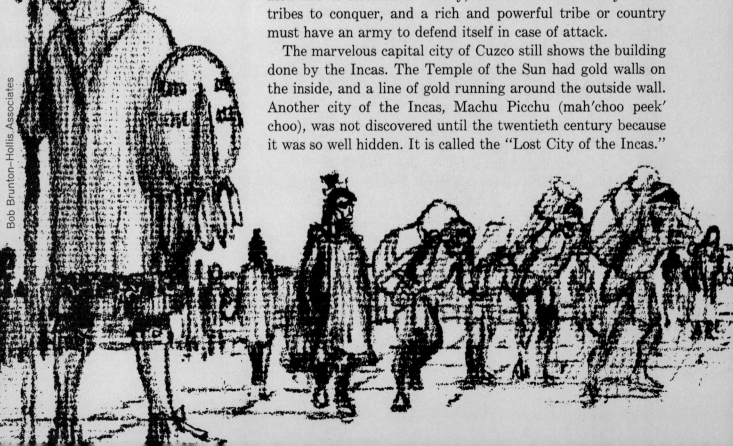

The Spaniards who came to the New World were looking for gold, silver, and precious stones. The Aztecs and the Incas had what they were looking for. Although both of these tribes had fought off other warring tribes, the Spanish were much more advanced. They were able to defeat both the Aztecs and the Incas. When they had done this, they destroyed many of their temples and palaces and took their gold, silver, and precious stones.

Drawing of the Aztec Temple of Quetzalcoatl near Mexico City

The Minoan Age

We now turn our attention back to the Mediterranean world—but now we will learn about the West. In this area would be brought together all the learning of the civilizations we have talked about so far. Man had come a long way from the simple cave life of old. Yet he was just beginning to develop countless other areas of life. In the West—on the island of Crete and in the country of Greece—this learning would be absorbed and transformed. Ancient civilizations—from Egyptian and Babylonian to the later Persian—would provide a variety of knowledge in the areas of art, industry, business, religion, literature, and government. From this knowledge the Greeks would pick those best suited to her needs and develop a civilization that would be the envy of the world.

All the time that civilization was developing in Egypt and in the land of the Persians, people who lived on the other side of the Mediterranean were also hard at work. These people were the Indo-Europeans who were to form the great Western civilization that we know today.

Look at the map and see where the Mediterranean Sea is and where Asia Minor and Greece are. See also where the Aegean Sea is. You can see that it is really part of the Mediterranean Sea. The little islands you see here are very important—especially the one named Crete (kreet).

Civilization started on the island of Crete very long ago. Since the people who lived there were surrounded by water, they learned to build ships and became very good sailors. They were sailors even before the Phoenicians were and they sailed the whole Mediterranean. They traded with the Egyptians and people of other great civilizations and learned many things.

These people were very good craftsmen and very good artists, too. In fact, they liked everything they used to be beautiful, even the big jars that they stored things in. So they painted pictures on them.

The Cretans were very wealthy and had beautiful jewelry and beautiful clothes. They had had a long time to collect these things by the time the Persians had built their empire, for civilization had started on the island of Crete even before the great pyramids of Egypt were built. People were living in Crete as long ago as 10,000 B.C. but, of course, they were not civilized then.

By 3000 B.C. these people were building houses and making things from copper and they were farming the land very well. And by 2000 B.C. they had become good craftsmen and artists. They traded their beautiful painted vases and bowls for other things. They soon learned that trade was good business and brought them great wealth. They did most of their trading by sea and sometimes became pirates. The kings of Crete were called the "sea kings."

The houses the people in Crete lived in were very beautiful and complicated. The outside walls were often painted pink or blue. The kings lived in a house with many rooms like an apartment. The walls were painted with beautiful pictures. Ruins of the Palace of Knossos (nahs′uss) still stand, and we can see the painted decorations and pictures on the walls. There are wide windows that were covered with a thin material in bad weather. There were even bathrooms in this magnificent palace!

The people of Crete liked sports very much and watched them and played at them often. Wrestling, boxing, dancing, and a kind of "acrobatic" bullfighting were especially popular.

There are many things about life in Crete that we would like to know, but we have found no written history. The Cretans did know how to write, but all we have found are clay tablets of bookkeeping.

The people of Crete influenced all the people who lived around the Aegean Sea. The whole civilization influenced by Crete is called the Minoan civilization. The *Minoan Age* lasted from about 3400 B.C. to 1100 B.C. Everything went very well for the Cretans until about 1400 B.C. At that time the beautiful cities on the island of Crete were destroyed. We do not know what destroyed these cities. It might have been an earthquake or it might have been a war.

The Minoan civilization found a new home in Greece. Some of the people from Crete may have moved there or their ideas and knowledge may have been passed on to other Indo-Europeans who were in that part of the world. We are not sure just how the civilization moved as it did.

The best-known town at that time was called Mycenae (my-see′nee). The Minoan civilization here came to be called the Mycenaean (my-seh-nee′uhn) civilization. Like other towns in that land, Mycenae was surrounded by a huge stone wall so that the people could protect themselves from anyone who might make war on them. Invaders were always coming into Greece, and there were many wars for a long time.

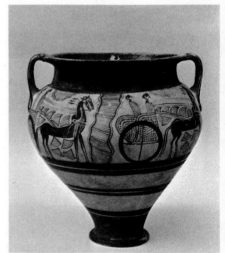

The Metropolitan Museum of Art, The Cesnola Collection; purchased by subscription, 1874-1876.

right: This Mycenaean vase shows one method of transportation

Ancient Greece

The way the land of Greece was shaped had a great deal to do with the way she developed, both economically and politically. Look at the map. You can see Greece is a peninsula surrounded on three sides by water. The land itself is crisscrossed by a series of mountains and dotted with many inlets and bays. See how the Gulf of Corinth almost completely separates the southern part of the peninsula from the northern section. We shall see later how these physical features caused people in each section of Greece to develop different ideas, customs, and ways of life.

This type of land was not easy to farm, and as more and more people came to the land, it became more difficult to raise enough food for all her people. So early in her history the mainland Greeks took to the sea. They began to trade with other lands around the Aegean Sea. Many of them settled in new lands and began to raise crops and build cities. These cities dotted the Mediterranean area. They continued to trade with their homeland. They sold goods they raised in the new area and bought other products from the various traders that frequented their shores.

These settlements were organized according to the system used by the Greeks at home. They were called city-states. This was a very special type of government. In a city-state people were loyal to one another. They were not necessarily loyal to other city-states in Greece or anywhere else. All of the Greek city-states together did form a kind of a single country but only because the people had the same history, worshipped the same gods, and had other things in common. At this time if you asked a man where he was from or what his nationality was, he would not say he was a Greek. He would say he belonged to a particular city-state. If he was from Athens he was an Athenian; if from Sparta, a Spartan; or if he was from Mycenae he was a Mycenaean.

opposite: Early Greek sailing vessel with one row of oars

left top: Ancient Greece and Crete

left bottom: Trading areas of Ancient Greeks and Phoenicians

But Greeks at first all were members of the same family. They were Indo-European invaders who came into Greece and made the country become very crowded, like the people who had gone into Persia. They came from the North. They began their conquest in about 1500 B.C. and ended it about 1200 B.C. They were very fierce fighters and killed many of the people

113

they found living in Greece. Those who were not killed intermarried with the invaders. Finally, all these people came to call themselves Hellenes (hell'eenz), after a legendary ancestor called Hellen. Later they came to be called Greeks, for this is what the Romans called them.

These people had learned much from Mycenaean civilization. They learned how to be craftsmen and they learned how to be artists; they built fine houses and wore beautiful clothes.

These Indo-European invaders kept their own language, though, and wrote some of the most wonderful poetry the world has ever read. The most famous of these poems are two that were written down by a man named Homer (ho'mer), a blind poet who lived about 800 B.C. The two poems were the *Iliad* (ill'ee-ahd) and the Odyssey (odd'ih-see). They were long poems, *epic poems*, about a famous war the Greeks were supposed to have fought long ago, and about what happened to some of the heroes after the war was over. These stories had been made up long before Homer was born. They were supposed to tell of things that really happened, but by the time Homer had heard them and wrote them down they had become more marvelous than anything that could actually have happened. They had not been written down hundreds of years before Homer's time because the Greeks didn't have an alphabet until they learned the Phoenician alphabet—and this was much later. Homer wrote down what he had heard as a boy about the war. He was an excellent writer and his works have become *classics;* that is, his poems were so good they are still read today.

In fact, thousands of years after Homer wrote his books they were proven to be more than just good stories. For in the late 1800's a German named Heinrich Schliemann used the information contained in the *Iliad* to help him discover the long-lost city of Troy; a few years later he found the city of Mycenae which we have told you about.

Homer's poems tell us much about how the early Greeks lived and what they thought. The Greeks learned from Homer about the gods, and came to believe in those he wrote about. These gods are very interesting; it seems they behaved more like people than like gods.

The Greeks thought of their gods as very powerful, people who were *immortal;* that is, they lived forever. The stories of their lives are very exciting.

The Greeks believed that all the gods lived on Mount Olympus (oh-lihm'puhs) and came down from time to time to visit men. According to the stories, the gods often got into mischief. They seemed to be less like gods than like human beings.

The chief god was Zeus (zooss), the god of thunder and lightning, the god of the sky. Zeus was the ruler of gods.

His daughter Athena (ah-thee'nah) was the guardian goddess who protected Greek cities, especially Athens. She was also the goddess of wisdom. It was said that Athena was born from the head of her father, Zeus, full grown and armed with shining weapons.

One of the most important and handsomest gods was Apollo (ah-pahl'oh) the god of the sun. The Greeks believed he drove the sun across the sky in his chariot every day. Apollo also was the god of youth, beauty, poetry, and music, and it was said that he could foretell the future.

Hera (hee'rah) was Zeus' queen—the queen of heaven. Poseidon (poh-sye'duhn), the god of the sea, ruled far below the waters. The goddess of love was Aphrodite (af-roh-dye'tee). Hermes (hur'meez), who wore winged sandals, was the messenger god.

The stories about the Greek gods are called *mythology* (mih-thal'oh-gee). The Greeks eventually began to build temples to honor their gods and goddesses, and priests performed all the religious ceremonies and helped the people decide what they must do to please the gods.

Some people in Greece were thought to have special powers. People called oracles (or'ah-k'lz) supposedly received messages directly from the gods. The priests had to sort out the oracles' meaning very often, however, for they usually spoke in riddles that were hard to understand.

All the people honored the gods on holidays, which were days of rest and feasting. In one city there were as many as seventy holidays every year! The Greeks' favorite way of honoring the gods on these days was to hold Olympic games or to give plays.

The Greeks were very fond of sports and had contests in the broad jump, the discus throw, javelin hurling, running, and wrestling. They also liked chariot races. People who won these events were given great honor. Poems were written about them and statues sometimes were made of them.

It was very important to be a good athlete in ancient Greece. People trained all year long to be in good condition to enter the Olympics or other games. The idea for the Olympic games

The Olympics date from 776 B.C. This girl is ready to participate in a race

115

that are held today came from the ancient Greeks, who held them as early as 776 B.C.

The plays the ancient Greeks gave to honor the gods were among the best ever written by anyone anywhere. The ones that have come down to us are still performed on the stage today.

All the things we have been talking about were things that the Greeks in different parts of the land had in common. But the city-states never did successfully co-operate with one another for a long period of time. They never became united into one country ruled by a single authority. This separateness was mostly caused by the land, which was full of mountains and had rugged coastlines. These things made it nearly impossible for the people to visit one another. The people could not build roads from one city-state to another, for they did not have the kind of equipment and machinery they needed to do this.

After the invasions of the Indo-Europeans, therefore, the various groups lost contact with each other. Each settlement grew into a community that was concerned only with its own affairs. Everything was done within the community. Its defense, its religious services, and its business were centered in the city. Each city became its own little nation or state. As time passed and the business of each growing community improved we shall see how these city-states actually began to compete with one another. Each one wanted to be the best and the richest city.

The Greek city-state included more than the town itself. It included all of the farmland that surrounded the town. Generally a farmer could walk to town within a few hours. Here he could enjoy the companionship of his fellow citizens and exchange news in the marketplace, or take part in the festivals or meetings that were always going on. The people living in such a city-state felt a great loyalty to their city and took great pride in the accomplishments of its citizens.

The citizens of each city-state were unwilling to give up or merge with other states. They believed they had everything they needed and saw no reason to live any other way. If they were organized into a large group of states they might lose some of their rights. This was something the independent city-states would not like to see happen.

Each city-state had some kind of government to keep order. The Greeks tried several different kinds of government. At first each city had a kind of king, or tribal chief. But as time went on the people who owned the land decided that they should and could rule better. They gradually gained power and by about 650 B.C. all the kings had either "given up" or had been turned out. Now the landowners ran the government. These people became what the Greeks called an *aristocracy* (air-is-tahk′rah-see). An aristocracy is a government by a small, privileged class who consider themselves best fit to rule. The aristocracy, as it turned out, were no fairer rulers than the kings had been. They owned most of the land and kept the peasants, most of whom were farmers, in poverty. Some of these peasants were forced to move to new lands to be able to live. Those who stayed, however, became poorer and poorer.

The government eventually began to be run by both the landowners and the rich artisans and traders in the city-state. The Greeks called this kind of government an oligarchy (ahl′ihgahrk-ee), which was still a government run by only a few, who were usually the wealthiest people in town.

Finally the Greeks arrived at a form of government they called a democracy (deh-moc′rah-see) because it was run by the *demos*, which was the Greek name for people.

Not every city-state came to be ruled by a democracy, however. Each city-state still was independent and did things in its own way. One city-state that was very different from the rest was called Sparta. It was one of the most famous of all Greek city-states found in the southern part of Greece.

The Spartans had taken over the land of Laconia, which was in the southern part of the Greek peninsula. A peninsula is a piece of land that is surrounded on nearly all sides by water. It is not quite an island because it is still connected to the mainland. This land of Laconia was in a part of Greece that was called Peloponnesus (pell-oh-puh-nee′suss). The Spartans did not have the whole peninsula, but only a part that was in the valley of a river called the Eurotas (you-roh′tuss). This area was surrounded on three sides by mountains and was easy to defend with soldiers.

When the population in Sparta started to grow and the land became very crowded the people decided to go to war and conquer other places near them. So from the eighth to the sixth century the Spartans conquered other peoples and took their lands rather than go to new areas and begin new cities as other Greek city-states had done.

In order to run this conquered territory the Spartans learned to use force. So they began to change. They re-organized their way of life entirely. By 600 B.C. the Spartans were living in a very hard and stern manner. They lived like soldiers and thought only of what was good for the state. Spartans believed that it was better to be physically strong and able to live in hardship than it was to live a pleasant, easy life. Spartan infants who were sickly were taken to the mountains and left to die. There was no room in military Sparta for anyone who was not physically strong.

All the men in Sparta were trained soldiers. When boys were seven years old, they began their military training. They were whipped and starved and treated very badly. This was to teach them to take any kind of hardship or punishment without crying. Later they went to live in barracks as soldiers. Spartan girls, also, were trained to be very strong for they were to produce healthy future soldiers for Sparta.

The Spartans were ruled by two kings and a council. All Spartans followed the rule of this government absolutely. There was no democracy. Most of the people ruled by the Spartans were kept in bondage; many were slaves. They lived and worked to provide supplies for the Spartans. As conquered people they had no say in the government and were guarded constantly by the Spartan army.

With this life the Spartan people became very rough and crude. They had none of the nicer things in life—no music or poetry, no lovely jewelry or clothing, no leisure time. Civilization seemed to be at a standstill in Sparta. The people did not want to have anything to do with outsiders. They did not carry on trade and did not visit outside their own land. They became very powerful but they did not have very much beauty or comfort in their lives. In war Sparta was a great success, but in everything else she was an absolute failure.

Another very famous city-state called Athens (ath′enz) was just the opposite. This city-state became a democracy, and her people loved beautiful things and wanted to know about the world outside. The ideas and ways of life developed in Athens are still important to us today.

Athens, like other city-states, had had kings until about 750 B.C. when the aristocracy had taken over. During this "Age of Nobles," in about 600 B.C., things became so very bad under the aristocracy that a man named Draco was chosen to make a set of rules for the Athenians to obey. In this way, the people would know at last where they stood. And they would have some rights. The rules Draco made were called the Code of Draco.

Draco's Code called for terrible punishments to anyone who broke the rules he made. If a man stole anything, even as small a thing as a loaf of bread, he was not just fined or sent to jail,

Vase showing two Greek gods in a contest

he was put to death! Draco explained the reason for such a severe law by saying that a thief deserved to be put to death.

You can understand how much trouble the laws of Draco caused. They were so hard that very soon afterward another man was called upon to make a new set of laws. This man was named Solon, which means "wise." His laws were very just and good. He made many reforms. He forbade selling people into slavery for their debts. Solon also allowed poor people to take part in the government, and he made the rich people pay their share of taxes. Solon was very important and did much to help Athens grow into a democracy.

Still some people were not satisfied with Solon's laws. The upper classes thought the laws gave too much to the lower classes and the lower classes thought they gave too much to the upper classes.

About 560 B.C. a man named Pisistratus (pie-sihs'trah-tuss) took charge. He was not elected or chosen by the people. He gathered a group of armed men together and made himself the ruler. No one could stop him because he was very powerful. There were others from time to time in Greece who did the same thing. Anyone who did this was called a *tyrant*. Nowadays only a ruler who is cruel and unjust is called a tyrant. Pisistratus, however, settled the difficulties of both sides, and he was neither cruel nor unjust.

Pisistratus ruled according to the laws of Solon. He broke up large estates and gave the land to the poor. He also began building projects to give more people work. He was a good tyrant, but his sons who inherited his position weren't. Finally, in about 510 B.C., the Athenians got tired of them and drove them out of Athens.

The next man to try to settle the quarrels between the two classes was named Clisthenes (klice'theh-neez). Clisthenes gave every citizen a vote and ruled wisely and well. He started the process of ostracism (ahs'trah-sihz-'m). If for any reason the people wanted to get rid of a man, all they had to do was scratch his name on any piece of broken pot or jar they might find and drop it in a voting-box on a certain day. If there were enough votes, the man would have to leave the city and stay away for ten years. This was called ostracism, and a man who was treated this way was said to be *ostracized*.

Clisthenes' other reforms changed Athens' government. It was now truly a democracy. The citizens took a direct part in making the laws. All the city officials were either chosen by

Vase showing
Greek runners

lot or elected, and they were responsible to the people. If they did not follow the people's wishes they could be taken out of office by the assembly of citizens.

The Greeks had accomplished much in their part of the world, and their influence spread to other areas on the coast of Italy and Spain. In the coming centuries the Greeks were to create and develop great art, literature, an important system of government, and—perhaps most importantly—great ideas.

But the future of Greece was not to be easy. The city-states would have to fight an outside force—the Persians. They also would engage in a great civil war that would alter drastically the history of Greece. Yet, during the hundreds of years of Greek power and prestige a degree of civilization was reached that far exceeded anything obtained in the Near East. In fact, the Greek civilization was so great that much of what was accomplished has never been equaled.

Rome Begins to Develop

Nobody really knows who were the first people living in Italy. Some were lake dwellers like the people in very early Switzerland. In about 2000 B.C. some Indo-European people came into the land and gave it their name. They were Italic tribesmen who took the central part of the land.

They did not all live in the same place, but each of the tribes took a different part of the land. The Latins were the most important of these Italic tribes. When Rome finally became established many, many years later, it was the language of these people that was used. This language of course was Latin.

The Italians were farmers who did very well in the new land. They did not know very much about civilization as yet, but they were very smart and could learn.

About the year 1000 B.C. a people called Etruscans came into the land. We don't know where they came from, but they were very highly civilized. They were good craftsmen and knew how to write and how to make very beautiful things. They settled very near the Italians and taught them about civilization.

The Italians were not traders, because they did not know very much about ships, but the Etruscans were traders. They moved around and learned new things and the Italians learned from them.

The Italians also learned from the Greeks, who had settled in the south of the land. These were some of the Greeks who had left Greece to find new lands. They were civilized people, as we have learned, and had much to teach the Italians.

In about 600 B.C. other invaders—the Celts—came into the central part of the land. The Celts had fair skin and blue eyes and were very good fighters who had given the Etruscans much trouble. They were really barbarians at that time. They finally moved into the north of the land, however, to a place that was then called Gaul; today we know it as France.

In about 1400 B.C. the Latins moved to a plain near the Tiber River. They had not lived there at the very first, because the plain had been a volcano and no one could live there. By 1400 B.C., however, the earth there was quiet again, and the

Ancient Italy

above: Bronze statue of an
Etruscan youth

right: Romulus and Remus
with the wolf

ground was very good for farming. So the Latins moved in and founded the city of Rome. Legends say that Rome was founded about 755 B.C., but we think it was earlier. Roman legend said that Rome was founded by a boy named Romulus (rah′mue-luhs). It said that he and his twin brother Remus (ree′muhs) were put into a little boat when they were babies and that they floated down the Tiber River until they came to the place that was to be Rome. Here the boat stopped. Both Romulus and Remus were just babies and they were without their mother.

The story says that a female wolf fed them and took care of them until a Latin farmer found them and took them to live in his house.

When the boys grew older Romulus marked off the city of Rome in the dirt with a stick. His brother Remus made fun of what he was doing and so Romulus killed him. Romulus, therefore, became the founder of Rome.

Romulus does not sound like a very nice boy, but that was the way the Romans told the story. And the name Rome came from the name Romulus.

Some other legends about the early history of the Latins were also told. These legends are probably not really history, but they were so interesting that the Latins handed the stories down from generation to generation. Finally, a poet named Vergil wrote them down in a poem called the *Aeneid* (eh-nee'ihd).

Rome became civilized mainly because of the Etruscans. It then became the most important town in Italy. At first, Rome was ruled by Etruscan kings, who had conquered the people in about 750 B.C. The last one was named Tarquin. The people finally drove him out of Rome in 509 B.C.

The Romans were very practical people. They were good at making laws and governing. They were not as good as the Greeks at writing plays or music or making other artistic things. They did not like to play the same games as Greeks played.

Their gods, however, were much like the Greek gods. In fact, they matched them pretty well. Their chief god was Jupiter. His wife was Juno. Ceres was the goddess of harvest, and Saturn was in charge of the time to begin planting. Mars, the god of war, was to be very important to the later Romans.

The Romans began to live a different kind of life from the one the early Latins had led. They became traders and learned about boats. They also began to build beautiful houses with many rooms and to make beautiful clothing and jewelry.

They learned from the Greeks how to build beautiful and impressive temples to their gods and they also built other public buildings. But all of this took a lot of time, hundreds of years. You have heard the saying that "Rome was not built in a day." It certainly was not. But once the city was built and the people began to prosper and be very civilized, they were to go on to do astonishing things in many parts of the world.

INDEX: *Young People's Story of the Ancient World, Prehistory to 500 B.C.*

Type   *Century Expanded*
Typesetter   *American Typesetting Corporation*
Printer   *The Regensteiner Corporation*